THE ROCK ENCYCLOPEDIA

BY A. W. BUCKEY

Encyclopedias

An Imprint of Abdo Reference
abdobooks.com

TABLE OF CONTENTS

ROCKS FORMED OUTSIDE THE ROCK CYCLE

WHAT IS A ROCK?

Rocks are not living things, but life depends on them. Rocks make up the outermost layer of Earth, or the crust. This is where humans and animals live. The crust is made from huge sheets of rock called tectonic plates. Sand, clay, pebbles, and mountains are all rocks of different sizes. Rocks are also found in outer space. Sometimes, rocks from space land on Earth.

Rocks have long been part of human life. Early humans made tools out of rocks. Today, rocks are used in buildings and machines. They are also found in homes and jewelry. Some rocks are used for artistic and religious purposes too.

Rocks come in a variety of shapes, colors, and patterns. A rock can be as small as a tiny clay particle or as large as a mountain. But all rocks have some things in common. One is that all rocks are solid. This means liquids and gases are not rocks. All rocks also consist of one or more minerals.

The minerals in granite often give the rock a colorful, speckled appearance.

Minerals are the building blocks of rocks. They are made up of one or more chemical elements. Minerals may contain just one type of atom. These minerals are called elements. Minerals may also contain multiple kinds of atoms bonded together. A mineral has a crystal structure. Its atoms are organized in a specific pattern. This structure shapes the mineral. Metals and gems are among the minerals that can be found in rocks.

Some rocks are made of just one mineral. For example, quartzite rocks are completely or almost completely made of quartz. However, many rocks contain combinations of different minerals. One example is granite. This common rock often contains several minerals, such as quartz, feldspar, and mica.

HOW ROCKS FORM

Rocks existed in outer space long before Earth formed. The first minerals came from stars that exploded in space. Stars are made of elements. Their explosions released some of these elements into space. Over time, the elements cooled into mineral dust. This dust gradually formed bigger and bigger clumps. These clumps became rocks. Some rocks got very large. In this way, asteroids and planets were created.

Scientists believe Earth formed more than 4.5 billion years ago. It formed when one small rocky planet, sometimes called early Earth, crashed into another. The heat from the crash turned the planet's surface into magma, a hot liquid that cools into rock. As the surface cooled, new rocks began to form. The planet became Earth. Scientists think this collision also formed the Moon.

THE FIRST ROCKS

The first rocks were made of just a few elements. Some of the earliest rocks contained the element carbon. Carbon consists of just one type of atom. Later, there were minerals made of more than one atom. One early mineral of this type is olivine. Olivine contains silicon, oxygen, and magnesium or iron. It is common in Earth's mantle, the layer below the crust. The first rocks on Earth were likely rich in olivine. They may have been very similar to komatiites, a rare type of rock.

THE ROCK CYCLE

There are three main types of rocks on Earth: igneous, metamorphic, and sedimentary. Each type of rock forms in a different way. Each is related to the others in a process called the rock cycle. Minerals travel through this cycle, changing into different types of rock.

The first rocks on Earth were igneous rocks. The word *igneous* means "from fire." These rocks are formed from the cooling of magma or lava. *Magma* is the word for this melted rock when it is under Earth's surface. When magma reaches the surface, it is known as lava. When a volcano erupts, lava comes out of it. The lava cools and hardens into igneous rock. The islands of Hawaii were created from this process.

Igneous rocks can also form far beneath Earth's surface. The tectonic plates on Earth's crust fit together like puzzle pieces. These plates pull and push against one another. When the

Igneous rocks that form from cooling lava on Earth's surface are often fine grained or glassy in texture.

plates shift, they can release magma inside Earth's crust. This magma solidifies into rock.

Over time, natural forces such as wind, rain, and friction wear rocks down. This process is known as weathering. As rocks weather, they break down into smaller and smaller pieces. These pieces can be easily carried or moved by air currents or running water. These smaller rocks become sediment, or solid material that is carried from one place to another.

The mud, sand, and silt at the mouth of a river are examples of sediment. Over time, layers of sediment build up. The pressure on the lower layers can fuse sediment together into a harder, more compact form. For example, sandstone often forms from layers of sand that is moved by water. These layers build up on shores and deltas. Over thousands of years, they become rock. Sediment can also lose water, becoming more solid. These are the ways sedimentary rock forms.

Sedimentary rock can also include materials from things that were once alive. One example is limestone. This sedimentary rock usually forms when the shells of marine creatures build up and combine. The islands of the Bahamas in the Caribbean Sea are made from limestone. New limestone is still forming there.

Sometimes intense pressure or heat change the mineral structures in a rock. Fluids such as water can also cause these changes. When this happens, a new rock called a metamorphic rock forms. This name comes from the word *metamorphosis*, which means "changing form." Metamorphic rocks change from one kind to another. Marble, a rock often used in sculptures and buildings, is one type of metamorphic rock. It forms from limestone that gets extremely hot. The heat causes the crystals in the limestone to grow larger. This change in structure gives the rock a different look and feel.

Minerals undergo all stages of the rock cycle. Igneous and metamorphic rocks can weather into sediment, forming sedimentary rocks. Both igneous and sedimentary rocks can change structure and become metamorphic rocks. And metamorphic and sedimentary rocks can liquify into magma, which forms igneous rocks. Changes in rocks often happen over very long stretches of time. These periods are measured using the geologic timescale.

Pure marble is typically white in color, but the metamorphic rock can come in other colors if impurities such as minerals are present when it forms.

GEOLOGIC TIMESCALE

The geologic timescale measures periods in Earth's history. People use it to understand changes in the planet and the atmosphere. It also gives a timeline for life on Earth. The scale begins with Earth's formation more than 4.5 billion years ago. It stretches into the present day.

The geologic timescale is divided into categories including eons. There have been four eons in Earth's history. The first three were the Hadean, Archean, and Proterozoic. Together, they make up the Precambrian Era. During the Hadean Eon, Earth's outer crust formed. This was a time of great tectonic activity. Hadean rocks either melted or sank into the mantle, which lies below the crust. The earliest rocks still in existence are from the Archean Eon. In the Proterozoic Eon, rocks made from carbon became common.

The current eon is the Phanerozoic. Eons are divided into eras. Eras last tens of millions to billions of years. So far, there have been three eras in the Phanerozoic: the Paleozoic, Mesozoic, and Cenozoic. During these eras, Earth's tectonic plates shifted. This formed continents and mountain ranges. Living things became part of the rock cycle too. Their skeletons and remains became part of sediment and rocks.

Eras are split into periods, which are divided into epochs. An epoch can last millions or tens of millions of years. The current epoch is the Holocene, which began 11,700 years ago. It marks the time in which humans have made major changes to Earth's environment. These include the use of many kinds of rocks. Humans have also created new rocks during this epoch.

EON	ERA	PERIOD	EPOCH	MYA*
Phanerozoic	Cenozoic	Quaternary	Holocene	0.01
			Pleistocene	2.6
		Neogene	Pliocene	5.3
			Miocene	23.0
		Paleogene	Oligocene	33.9
			Eocene	56.0
			Paleocene	66.0
	Mesozoic	Cretaceous		145.0
		Jurassic		201.3
		Triassic		251.9
	Paleozoic	Permian		298.9
		Pennsylvanian		323.2
		Mississippian		358.9
		Devonian		419.2
		Silurian		443.8
		Ordovician		485.4
		Cambrian		541.0
Proterozoic Archean Hadean	Precambrian			2500
				4000
				4600

***Million Years Ago**

11

ADAKITE

Adakite is a rare type of rock that is usually gray, black, or brown in color. Scientists believe it forms between tectonic plates. Many tectonic plates meet on the ocean floor. When these plates collide, rock from one plate sometimes goes underneath the other. This is called subduction. Heat and pressure from subduction can cause rocks to melt. Then they cool into new igneous rocks. Adakite is one of those rocks.

Adakite can also form in other ways. It can be both an extrusive and intrusive igneous rock. An extrusive igneous rock forms from lava cooling aboveground. An intrusive igneous rock forms when magma solidifies underground. Adakite is named after Adak, the place where it was first found. Adak is part of a chain of volcanic islands located between Russia and Alaska.

Adak Island, which is part of the Aleutian Islands, is home to several volcanoes. Adakite rocks form as a result of volcanic activity on the island.

Cerro Mackay, a mountain in Chile, consists of adakite columns.

A FINE-GRAINED ROCK

Adakite is a fine-grained igneous rock. Fine-grained rocks have small mineral crystals. Coarse-grained rocks have large mineral crystals, while medium-grained rocks are in between. In general, igneous rocks that cool more slowly are coarser grained. Igneous rocks that cool more quickly are finer grained. This is because a slower cooling time gives the crystals in the rock more time to grow. Scientists think adakite is very similar to the first rocks in Earth's crust. They use adakite to study how the crust may have formed.

DID YOU KNOW?

Intrusive igneous rocks are also called plutonic rocks. This name comes from Pluto, the Roman god of the underworld.

Andesite rocks often have a speckled or spotted surface.

ANDESITE

Andesite is an extrusive igneous rock. It ranges in color from light to dark gray and is fine grained. In general, extrusive igneous rocks are more likely to be fine grained. This is because lava cools more quickly at Earth's surface than magma does underground. Earth's atmosphere speeds up the cooling process.

The Ollagüe volcano, located in the Andes Mountains, is known for having andesite lava flows.

RICH IN FELDSPAR

Andesite rocks contain a lot of feldspar. Feldspar is a very common mineral. It is made from the element aluminum and the compound silica, which is a mixture of silicon and oxygen. Andesite can also contain other minerals such as mica and pyroxene. Not all andesites have the same minerals in the same amounts. As a result, andesites vary in color and appearance.

Andesite is named after the Andes Mountains in South America, where the rock is often found. Today, andesites are used in construction. They can be used as pavement material and as gravestones.

DID YOU KNOW?

More than half of Earth's crust is made of feldspar minerals.

APLITE

Aplites are intrusive igneous rocks. The name *aplite* comes from the Greek word for "simple." Aplites are considered simple because they contain only a few minerals. The most common type of aplite is granitic aplite. It is made of quartz and feldspar. Quartz is a mineral made of silica. It is commonly found in rocks. Pure quartz is clear in color. But small amounts of other minerals can give quartz other colors.

LIGHT-COLORED, MEDIUM-GRAINED

Aplite is a medium-grained rock. Its texture looks like sugar. Aplites are light-colored rocks and are usually just one color. This is because there are so few minerals in the rock. They do not contrast with one another. They don't form chunks with different colors or textures.

Aplites sometimes form as dikes. These are vertical stripes of rock. They form when magma travels upward and fills in cracks between rocks. Dikes can be as thin as a few centimeters. Others are many meters wide. Aplite is used to make ceramic tiles. It is also used to make glass.

The presence of certain minerals in aplite, such as feldspar, can make the rock appear pinkish in color.

Aplite dikes often appear as stripes or veins that cut across other rocks.
Dikes

Hāʻena Beach on Kauai, Hawaii, is home to basaltic rocks, boulders, and cliffs.

BASALT

Basalt is a fine-grained, dark-colored rock. It is usually made from combinations of the minerals pyroxene and feldspar. The components of andesite and basalt are similar. But basalt has a finer grain than andesite. It also contains less silica.

Basalts form when lava or magma cools very quickly. One example is pillow basalt. Pillow basalts form when volcanoes erupt underwater. When this happens, the magma that touches the water cools and solidifies. The magma inside stays in liquid form, and as the outside solidifies, the effect is like blowing into a balloon. The resulting basalts have soft, rounded shapes that resemble pillows.

AN ABUNDANT ROCK

Almost all of Earth's ocean floor consists of basaltic rock. Hawaii's largest island is made from a basaltic volcano. Basalts can also form on other planets. Most of Venus and Mars are covered in basalt. Volcanoes on these planets produced the rock.

Today, basalt is used for many purposes. It is often crushed and mixed with other rocks to make the material used for roads. Basalt may also be used for buildings, tiles, and paving stones. There are large basalt mines in Germany, Armenia, and the United States.

The Olympic Mons volcano on Mars is made of basalt. It is the largest volcano in the solar system.

BLAIRMORITE

Blairmorite is a rare type of extrusive igneous rock. It can be found in Alberta, Canada. It is also present in Mozambique, a country in southeastern Africa. Blairmorite formed from an unusual type of lava. The volcano that created the blairmorite in Canada erupted about 100 million years ago.

PHENOCRYSTS IN BLAIRMORITE

Blairmorite has a spotted appearance. The rock is green in color with chunks of reddish minerals inside. These minerals are called phenocrysts.

When volcanoes erupt underground, their magma cools slowly. The crystals that form are coarse grained. Sometimes, a partly cooled magma flow travels aboveground.

Blairmorite is named after Blairmore, a town in Alberta, Canada. The rock comes from the area's Crowsnest Formation.

When this happens, the lava starts to cool faster. The rapidly cooled lava is finer grained. It forms rocks with phenocrysts. These slower-cooled crystals stay trapped inside the quickly cooled rock. This surrounding rock is called the groundmass or rock matrix. Rocks with phenocrysts are known as porphyritic.

Most phenocrysts in blairmorite are made of a mineral called analcime. But the rock may also contain garnet or other minerals. The groundmass and phenocrysts are made from the same minerals. But they look different from one another. This is because the speed at which a mineral cools affects its crystal structure.

Analcime, a major component of blairmorite, sometimes forms into rounded crystals with flat faces.

Carbonatites range in color from light gray to yellow.

CARBONATITE

Carbonatite is a type of igneous rock. There are two main types of igneous rocks. Felsic igneous rocks contain lots of feldspar and silica, while mafic rocks contain magnesium and iron. But carbonatite is different from most igneous rocks. It is made of more than 50 percent carbonate, which is a combination of carbon and oxygen. Carbonatite rocks can look very different depending on which minerals they contain.

Carbonate magmas come from Earth's mantle. This is the layer of rock below the crust. The mantle is much thicker than the crust. It is about 1,800 miles (2,900 km) thick. In contrast,

CHEMICAL COMPOSITION

Chemicals are materials with a defined composition. They consist of certain elements that are bonded together in specific ratios and patterns. All minerals have a chemical composition. These compositions are represented by symbols. For example, the symbols for carbonate are CO_3^{2-}. This represents the ratios of elements and how they are bonded. One carbon atom (C) and three oxygen atoms (O_3) are bonded together, along with two electrons ($^{2-}$).

the crust is about 25 miles (40 km) thick. It is thinner in some places than in others.

SOURCE OF RARE EARTH ELEMENTS

Carbonatites are a source of rare earth elements (REEs) such as cerium and lanthanum. REEs are a small set of elements that are not commonly found in concentrated deposits, which makes them harder to mine and process. REEs have many uses in high-tech products. Cars, phones, TVs, and computers all contain REEs. For this reason, people mine and quarry carbonatite deposits.

Cerium extracted from carbonatites can be used in products such as flat-screen TVs.

DIORITE

Diorite is an intrusive igneous rock. This dark-colored, coarse-grained rock is very similar to andesite. It differs in that it forms underground instead of aboveground. Diorite is made mostly of feldspar. It can also contain other minerals such as hornblende and biotite.

Diorite rocks often have a speckled "salt and pepper" color.

Sacsayhuamán, an ancient Inca fortress in Peru, is home to a natural diorite rock formation called the Rodadero. Visitors can slide down the formation.

FORMATION IN DIKES AND SILLS

Like andesite, diorite sometimes occurs in dikes. Diorites can also form in sills. Sills form when magma cools between layers of rock. This results in horizontal stripes of different rocks. Some sills are extremely thin. Others can be hundreds of feet thick. They can stretch for many miles. The Inca people of South America once used diorite as a building stone. Today, the rock is still used in construction. It is a material for pavement, curbs, and buildings.

Dolerite, which is typically gray or black in color, is often used as a construction material.

DOLERITE

Dolerite, sometimes called diabase, is an intrusive rock. It is very similar to basalt and gabbro. These rocks consist of the same minerals. But dolerite is coarser grained than basalt and finer grained than gabbro.

Like many other igneous rocks, dolerite is often found in dikes and sills. Sills and dikes can help geologists learn about the history of rocks. They show the histories of volcanic eruptions. Geologists can study sills and dikes to determine the ages of different rocks.

A HARD ROCK

Dolerite is a very hard rock. Hard rocks do not scratch easily. People can use hard rocks for many purposes. In ancient Egypt, people used dolerites as rock pounders. They built large structures out of rocks such as granite. They used dolerite tools to break and shape the granite stones.

THE MOHS SCALE

The Mohs scale is used to rank minerals based on their level of hardness. The scale was created by a German mineralogist in the 1800s. It measures how easy a rock is to scratch. The scale ranges from 1 to 10, with 1 being the softest and 10 being the hardest. A human fingernail has a Mohs rating of about 2.5, while a steel nail rates about 6.5. The hardest mineral on the scale is diamond, which rates 10. The softest is talc, which rates 1. Dolerite rates between 6 and 7.

Archaeologists have discovered some ancient Egyptian statues made of dolerite.

DUNITE

Dunite is an intrusive igneous rock that is usually light green in color. It is a type of peridotite. These are rocks that contain olivine. Olivine is a category of minerals that contain magnesium and silica. It is the most common mineral type in the mantle. Dunite rocks consist of more than 90 percent olivine. They come from Earth's mantle. Dunite is named after Dun Mountain in New Zealand. This mountain is made mostly of dunite.

Dunite is a durable and coarse-grained rock. It has a Mohs rating of 6.5 to 7.

SOURCE OF CHROMITE

Dunite is a major source of chromite, a metallic mineral. Metals are substances that conduct heat and electricity. They also reflect light. Some metals are soft and bendable. Many rocks contain metals. Rocks that contain valuable minerals, metals, or gems are called ores.

Chromite is used to produce chromium. People often use chromium to make metals shinier and stronger. A chrome-plated car, for example, has a glossy, polished finish.

ESSEXITE

Essexite is a type of gabbro. This rock is commonly found in North America and Europe. In order to be essexite, a rock must contain nepheline. This is part of a group of minerals called feldspathoids. These minerals are similar to feldspars but differ in that they do not contain as much silica.

The magma that creates essexite forms as a result of partial melting. Partial melting happens when only part of a solid rock turns to liquid. Some minerals melt faster than others. This means that melting changes the mineral composition and structure of a rock. A partially melted rock will have different minerals than a fully melted one. Essexite usually comes from rocks that are less than 10 percent melted.

A BUILDING AND CONSTRUCTION STONE

Essexite can be used in stones for buildings and pavement. Hard, durable rocks such as essexite are well suited for this purpose. A building stone must be able to withstand weathering and friction. Like other igneous rocks, essexite is also sometimes used to make tables and countertops.

Craigleith Island, located off the coast of Scotland, is composed entirely of essexite.

GABBRO

Gabbro is a dark-colored rock that has the same components as basalt. Both rocks are made mostly of feldspar and pyroxene. But unlike basalt, gabbro is an intrusive rock. It is also coarser grained than basalt. Essexite is one type of gabbro.

People mine gabbro rock deposits for chromium, nickel, and platinum. One of the world's biggest gabbro deposits is in Minnesota. Around 1.1 billion years ago, tectonic plates in the middle of what are now the United States and Canada pulled apart. The resulting split is known as the Midcontinent Rift. Magma intruded upward from the rift, forming new igneous rock.

THE DULUTH COMPLEX

Rock from the Midcontinent Rift created the Duluth Complex. This is a geological area in Minnesota that features a collection of rock deposits. The gabbro in the Duluth Complex formed in layers. The oldest layers are at the top of the complex. They were pushed upward by newer layers of rock.

Gabbro is named after a village in Tuscany, Italy.

There are also xenoliths inside the gabbro layers. Xenoliths are solid rocks carried by magma or lava flows. As the magma cools, new rock forms around the xenoliths. The xenoliths become fixed inside the new rock.

GRANITE

Granite is the most common igneous rock on Earth's surface. This intrusive, coarse-grained rock is formed from feldspar and quartz. Because these minerals are so common, granite is widespread. The rock's coarse grains often make it appear speckled or spotted.

Granite forms most of Earth's upper crust. It is also at the core of large mountain ranges such as the Himalayas and the Andes. This means that granite forms the base, or bottom, rock. Other layers of rock may lie above it or be mixed with it.

A USEFUL ROCK

Granite is a hard rock, rating about 6 to 7 on the Mohs scale. It is well known for its use as a building and construction material. Countertops are often made of granite. So are stone buildings. Granite is also a popular material for making tombstones.

The US state of New Hampshire is called the Granite State. This is because the state was once known for its many granite quarries. Today, the United States is still a major granite supplier. Every state except Delaware has granite quarries.

The Rock of Ages granite quarry in Graniteville, Vermont, has operated since the late 1800s.

HARZBURGITE

Harzburgite is a type of peridotite. It is an intrusive igneous rock. Unlike many other igneous rocks, it does not contain feldspar. But it can contain small amounts of garnet. Harzburgite is an ultramafic rock. These rocks have high amounts of magnesium and iron. Mafic rocks are usually dark in color too. Harzburgite has a dark green or black color. It is named after the Harz mountain range in Germany, where the rock is commonly found. Harzburgite is also found in Africa and Asia.

Harzburgite can contain minerals such as spinel, ilmenite, and magnetite.

FORMATION IN THE MANTLE

Harzburgite forms in Earth's mantle. It is created by the partial melting of other igneous rocks. This partial melting creates magma that then resolidifies. However, due to tectonic shifts, there are harzburgite rocks on Earth's surface. When the rock comes in contact with the air, it turns reddish brown. This is because the minerals within the rock oxidize. The oxygen in the air changes their chemical makeup. Like dunite, harzburgite is a source of chromite for chromium.

Icelandite was first discovered in Iceland's Þingvellir valley region. The Mid-Atlantic Ridge passes through this area.

ICELANDITE

Icelandite is an igneous rock that can be intrusive or extrusive. It is known as an intermediate volcanic rock. This means its silica content is in the middle range for volcanic rocks. The rock contains phenocrysts of several different minerals. Icelandite is considered a rare rock. Fragments of the rock are sometimes sold as collector's items.

A VOLCANIC ROCK

Icelandite is named after Iceland, an island country in northwestern Europe. Iceland is located on the boundary of two tectonic plates. This area is called the Mid-Atlantic Ridge. Iceland was formed by volcanic eruptions that occurred along the ridge about 150 million to 90 million years ago. Icelandite is one of the rocks formed by these eruptions. Eruptions still happen on the island today.

But icelandite is found in other places too. This is because volcanoes can form wherever there are cracks in Earth's crust. The US state of Oregon, for example, lies on a tectonic plate boundary. There are many volcanoes there. Icelandite can be found in the state.

Icelandite lava flows can be found in the Columbia River Basalt Group, which covers parts of several northwestern US states.

IGNIMBRITE

Ignimbrite is an extrusive volcanic rock. It is also called ignimbritic tuff or ash-flow tuff. Tuff is formed from volcanic ash. When volcanoes erupt, they release more than just lava. They also release gases, dust, and ash. When these substances cool and harden together, they become tuff.

A PYROCLASTIC ROCK

The flow of magma in a volcano can pick up and carry surrounding rocks. A magma flow with these surrounding rocks in it is known as a pyroclastic flow. Igneous rocks that contain these rock fragments, or pyroclasts, are called pyroclastic rocks. Ignimbrite is a pyroclastic tuff. It is cooled tuff that has been mixed with pyroclasts. Ignimbrite usually has vitric, or glass, shards. It can consist of many different minerals. Its makeup depends on the types of rocks present in a pyroclastic flow. This means ignimbrites can differ in appearance.

Ignimbrites vary widely in color and mineral composition. Many are brown, white, or gray.

But most ignimbrites usually have a rock called pumice in them.

The layers in ignimbrite make it easy to separate the rock into slabs. The rock is sometimes used in paving. Flagstones are sometimes made from ignimbrite.

Diamond-bearing kimberlites often form in vertical, pipe-like channels in the ground. These kimberlite pipes form as a result of volcanic activity.

KIMBERLITE

Kimberlite, an intrusive igneous rock, is formed by magma from Earth's mantle. It is created by the intrusion of magma into dikes, tunnels, and sills. Kimberlite is porphyritic, with many phenocrysts inside its groundmass. It is rich in olivine.

A DIAMOND SOURCE

Kimberlite is famous for being a diamond source. There are more than 6,500 kimberlite deposits worldwide, and most do not contain diamonds. However, more diamonds are found inside kimberlite than in any other rock in the world. Diamonds are minerals of pure carbon. The arrangement of their carbon atoms makes diamonds extremely hard. They are the hardest substance on Earth. This means a diamond can scratch any other material. But only a diamond can scratch another diamond.

Diamonds are considered very valuable. Their hardness makes them useful in tools such as drill bits. They are also prized as expensive jewels. People mine kimberlite deposits in order to find diamonds. The rock's name comes from that of a famous diamond mining town in South Africa.

Kimberlite is named after Kimberley, South Africa. The town was once home to a large kimberlite mine.

The spinifex texture of komatiites can vary in size and shape. Some rocks feature large, spiny plates, while others have smaller crystals.

KOMATIITES

Komatiites are some of the oldest rocks on Earth. They are ultramafic volcanic rocks. Most komatiites formed during the Archean Eon, which lasted from 4 to 2.5 billion years ago. The first life appeared on Earth during this time. Very few rocks on Earth come from before the Archean Eon. Before this time, Earth's crust was still forming. Many volcanic eruptions occurred during the Archean Eon. Gases from these eruptions helped create Earth's atmosphere. The eruptions also created rocks such as komatiites.

PLANT-LIKE CRYSTAL STRUCTURE

Geologists named komatiites after the Komati River in South Africa. This is where the first komatiites were found, in 1969. The olivines in komatiites have an unusual crystal structure. They are arranged in a spinifex texture. The olivine phenocrysts look like long, thin spikes of grass. The geologists who discovered komatiites thought this texture looked similar to the grassy spinifex plant.

Komatiites are known for containing high levels of magnesium and low levels of silica.

MOONSTONE

Feldspar is a common mineral. It comes in many different forms. Moonstone is made of two types of feldspar. Moonstone is found in both igneous and metamorphic rocks. Granite and pegmatite can contain moonstone.

Moonstone is typically milky white with a blue schiller, or shine. Different rocks have different types of schiller. Moonstone's schiller resembles moonlight. Schiller happens as a result of microscopic crystals of one mineral layered with a second mineral. The two layers reflect light differently because of their different structures. This makes moonstone appear to glow from within.

Moonstone's glowing appearance is due to an optical effect called adularescence.

Moonstones are often used in jewelry such as rings, necklaces, and earrings.

A GLOWING GEMSTONE

Moonstone is often sold as a gemstone. It is mined in southern Asia, eastern Africa, Madagascar, and the United States. Most moonstone comes from Sri Lanka, an island country in southern Asia. Moonstone is a birthstone for the month of June. It is also associated with the Cancer zodiac sign. The gem's glowing quality is said to represent inner growth. Some people believe moonstones have healing properties.

DID YOU KNOW?

Moonstone has layers composed mainly of two types of feldspar, orthoclase and albite.

Nakhlites are believed to have formed from basaltic magma on Mars about 1.3 billion years ago.

NAKHLITE

At 9:00 a.m. on June 28, 1911, people in northern Egypt saw a meteorite fall from the sky. The space rock landed near a village called El Nakhla El Bahariya. The people who saw the rock fall knew that it came from space. It took geologists time to determine that the rock was from the planet Mars. It was named nakhlite, after the village near which it was found.

More than 20 nakhlite meteorites had been found by 2025. All are igneous rocks. But they come from volcanoes on Mars, not on Earth. They are basaltic rocks that are rich in a type of pyroxene called augite. Augite is found in many dark-colored igneous rocks, including gabbro and andesites. It is also found in Moon rocks.

NAKHLITES AND THE HISTORY OF MARS

Nakhlites provide clues about Mars's history. The rocks' structure and makeup have been changed by water. Around 600 million years ago, water flowed through these rocks. The nakhlites also contain clay minerals, suggesting that they once mixed with water. This is evidence that there was once water on Mars.

MISTAKEN FOR METEORITES

Some rocks appear to be meteorites but are actually Earth rocks. Meteorites tend to be dark, heavy, and magnetic. People may think of meteorites as having pockmark-like holes. But meteorites usually do not have holes in them. One sign of a true meteorite is a fusion crust. This is a thin, glassy, brown or black crust on the rock's outer surface. It forms as the meteorite travels through Earth's atmosphere.

The 1911 nakhlite meteorite is one of more than 30 meteorites that are known to have come from Mars.

NEPHELINE SYENITE

Syenite is a type of intrusive igneous rock. Like other intrusive igneous rocks, it is coarse or medium grained. It consists of alkali feldspar, a type of feldspar rich in sodium and potassium, combined with another mineral. Nepheline syenite is made mostly of nepheline and feldspar. Nepheline syenites are not especially common, but they can be found all around the world.

Nepheline syenite rates 6 to 6.5 on the Mohs scale.

Nepheline syenite is commonly used in roofing granules, which provide texture and protection to roof shingles.

Many geologists are interested in nepheline syenites. This is because the rocks vary widely. They can have different makeups, and they may look and feel very different from one another. Geologists study nepheline syenites to figure out where these differences come from.

GLASS, ROOFS, AND ASPHALT

Nepheline syenite is used to whiten clay and make ceramics and glass. It is also used as a roofing material. The rock is often crushed and put in asphalt and concrete. Nepheline syenite is a source of rare minerals too. It is mined in places such as Canada and Norway.

Obsidian has a conchoidal fracture. This means that when the rock breaks, its surfaces are curved, smooth, and sharp edged.

OBSIDIAN

Obsidian is a volcanic glass. Glass is a solid that does not have a crystal structure. The kind of glass that people use in everyday life is often made of rocks such as sand or limestone. But if magma and lava cool very quickly, they can also form glass. Obsidian is an unusual rock because it does not have a crystal structure. However, it can contain microscopic crystals called crystallites. It can also contain some phenocrysts.

A SHINING, BLACK WEAPON

Obsidian is a little harder than everyday glass. It is known for its shine and black color. Obsidian can also come in other colors, such as green and gray.

Throughout history, many cultures have made weapons and tools out of obsidian. Archaeologists have found obsidian tools in Ethiopia that date back 1.7 million years. By about 200,000 years ago, humans were trading obsidian across long distances. The ancient Greeks and the Aztecs made obsidian mirrors. Today, obsidian is sometimes used as a gemstone.

Early humans used obsidian to make durable tools such as arrowpoints, knives, and scrapers.

PĀHOEHOE BASALT

Pāhoehoe basalt is a type of basalt. The word *pāhoehoe* is Hawaiian. There are six active volcanoes on the Hawaiian Islands, so volcanic eruptions are common there.

The Hawaiian language has names for different types of lava flows. Lava known as 'a'ā is quick flowing, thick, and rough. It contains large chunks. Pāhoehoe lava is hotter and runnier. It flows more slowly. Pāhoehoe lava has a ropy look, like strands twisting together. Smaller flows called toes can form within this lava mass. Pāhoehoe lava erupts at a heat of about 2,100 degrees Fahrenheit (1,150°C), but it cools very quickly in the air. It hardens into pāhoehoe basalt.

As pāhoehoe lava flows, its crust begins to harden while the liquid lava underneath keeps moving. This forms undulating wrinkles and folds of pāhoehoe basalt.

A DARK, ROPY ROCK

Pāhoehoe basalt is dark colored. It often has the same ropy texture as the lava flow from which it forms. Pāhoehoe basalts are less common than pillow basalts. This is because pillow basalts form at ocean ridges, which are more common than aboveground volcanoes. But both forms of basalt are more common than 'a'ā flows.

Pegmatites can contain a variety of valuable minerals, including spodumene, beryl, and tourmaline.

PEGMATITE

Pegmatites are extremely coarse-grained intrusive igneous rocks. The crystals in pegmatites are very large, measuring about 0.4 inches (1 cm) or more across. Usually, pegmatites are granite. But other coarse-grained rocks can be pegmatites too.

Pegmatites form in the last stage of magma crystallization. During the crystallization process, elements inside a magma flow join together and create minerals. Some minerals in the magma form quickly. Others take more time. But water within the magma does not crystallize. Instead, it collects inside the magma. Types of atoms called ions move around inside pockets of this hot water. The ions come together to make large crystals. This is how pegmatite is created.

BIG CRYSTALS

Pegmatite crystals can be extremely large. One famous piece of pegmatite in South Dakota contained a giant crystal of spodumene, which is a lithium source. The crystal was 42 feet (13 m) long. Lithium is commonly used in batteries. It is also used as an ingredient in mood disorder medications.

Pure spodumene is typically white or colorless, but the mineral can also occur in shades of pink, yellow, green, and purple.

PUMICE

Like obsidian, pumice is a kind of volcanic glass. It forms when lava or magma cools extremely quickly. But pumice and obsidian have different textures. Pumice forms from a pyroclastic flow. When the flow solidifies, it releases gases that are trapped inside. The gases escape, leaving many holes in the rock. This forms a rock with a light, frothy texture. The word *pumice* comes from a Latin word for "foam." In contrast, the gases in obsidian are dissolved in the rock. This gives obsidian its smooth, solid surface.

A SCRUBBING STONE

Pumice is often light in color. It is often used as an ingredient in concrete. The rock's rough texture also makes it useful as an abrasive. An abrasive wears down other

Many pumice rocks are so light that they can float on water.

Pumice is often used in beauty products such as exfoliants, foot scrubbers, and sponges.

materials through friction. For example, people use pumice stones to soften calluses on their skin.

Pumice is also used to create stonewashed jeans. During this process, jeans are washed for an hour or more alongside stones. The stones wear on the jeans, giving them a faded appearance. Pumice is also commonly found in products such as erasers and pet litter.

Rhyolite contains high amounts of silica. It comes in a range of colors, including light gray, pink, and tan.

RHYOLITE

Rhyolite's chemical makeup is similar to that of granite. Both rocks contain feldspar and quartz in similar ratios. However, rhyolite is an extrusive rock, while granite is intrusive. Because extrusive rocks cool faster than intrusive ones, rhyolite has a much smaller crystal structure than granite.

Rhyolite's groundmass is either glassy or fine grained. But the rock contains phenocrysts of quartz and feldspar. These can form when magma starts to cool underground and then finishes cooling after a volcanic eruption. Like granite, rhyolite is found all over the world.

A VUGGY ROCK

Because rhyolite cools quickly, the rock sometimes forms
gas pockets known as vugs. Later, water and gas move
through these holes. New crystals, including ones that create
gemstones, may form inside the vugs. Vuggy rhyolite is
highly valued for this reason. People hope to find gems inside
the rock.

Landmannalaugar, Iceland,
is known for its colorful
rhyolite mountains.

SHONKINITE

Shonkinite is an intrusive igneous rock. It is a dark-colored variety of syenite. Shonkinite contains feldspar and augite. The augite gives the rock its dark color. Shonkinite is named after the place in Montana where it was first discovered. There, the rock forms most of the Shonkin Sag laccolith.

SHONKINITE IN LACCOLITHS

Laccoliths are dome-like rock structures under Earth's surface. They form when magma travels upward through Earth's crust. The upward flow of magma pushes up existing rock, creating a dome shape. The flow stops before it reaches the surface. But the rock layers covering a laccolith can wear away over time.

Shonkinite is a coarse-grained rock. In addition to feldspar and augite, it can contain minerals such as biotite and olivine.

The Shonkin Sag is located along Montana's Highwood Mountains. It is home to Lost Lake, which is surrounded by walls of shonkinite rock.

The result is a laccolith mountain. Utah's Henry Mountains are laccolith mountains.

Montana's Shonkin Sag laccolith measures about 1 mile (1.6 km) wide and 197 feet (60 m) thick. It contains rocks such as diorite, granite, and pegmatite. These rocks formed about 48 to 60 million years ago. Today, shonkinite is used for construction projects and roads. Shonkinite has also been used to build dams.

TRACHYTE

Trachyte is a fine-grained igneous rock. It is usually light colored. Trachyte is composed of mostly feldspar. Its mineral composition is similar to that of syenite. However, trachyte is an extrusive volcanic rock, while syenite is intrusive. The rock's rough texture inspired its name. *Trachyte* comes from the Greek word *trachys*, which means "rough." Trachyte is often a porphyritic rock with phenocrysts inside.

THICK LAVA FLOWS

Trachyte comes from thick lava flows. Two examples of trachyte volcanoes are Mount Kilimanjaro in Tanzania and Mount Erebus in Antarctica. Trachyte sometimes has a banded, streaky appearance. These bands correspond to the flow of the lava as it cooled.

Trachyte is commonly used in building and construction. The stone is found on all continents. It has been mined in northern Italy for thousands of years. The ancient Romans used trachyte in many of their buildings.

Trachyte rocks often have large crystals of minerals such as sanidine embedded inside them.

The trachyte volcano Mount Kilimanjaro is the tallest mountain in Africa. It includes three volcanic cones: Kibo, Mawenzi, and Shira.

TUFF

Tuff is solidified volcanic ash, dust, and gases. Different tuffs form from different ash flows. Vitric tuff is glass, while crystal tuff contains crystal chips. Lithic tuff has rocks in it. Volcanic ash can erupt from cracks in Earth's crust. This can also create tuff.

CARVING AND SCULPTING

Tuff is a soft rock. For this reason, it is frequently used in carving and sculpting. The famous Moai statues of Easter Island are made from tuff.

The textures, colors, and compositions of tuff can vary widely. Some types include crystal tuff, ash-fall tuff, and pumiceous tuff.

Easter Island, also known as Rapa Nui, is a volcanic island in the southern Pacific Ocean. Its landmass is made mostly of tuff. The Rapa Nui people used this rock to make Moai, or large stone busts. These busts represent their ancestors. They are made from tuff blocks that weigh 82 short tons (74 metric tons). The tallest statue is about 33 feet (10 m) tall.

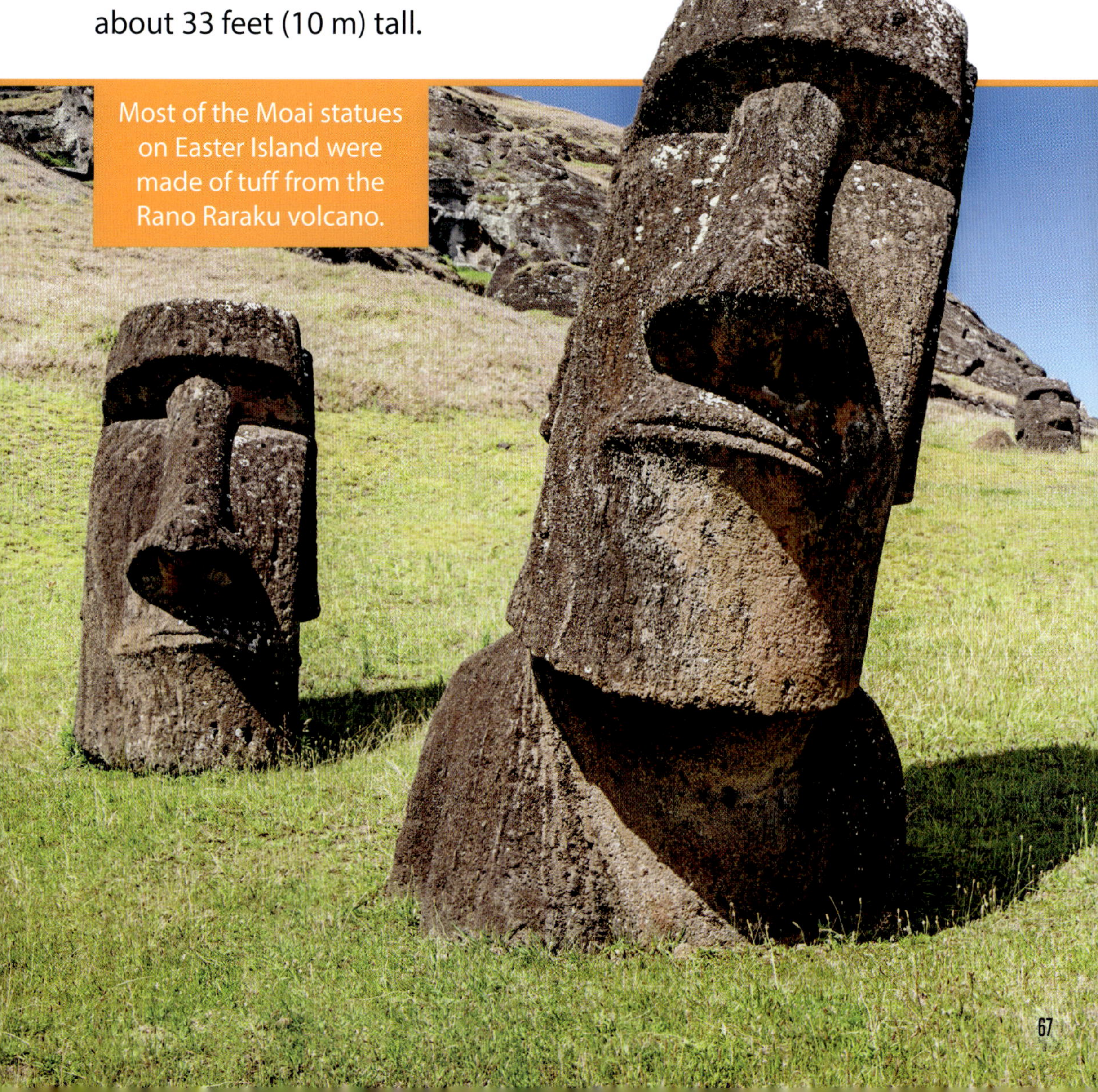

Most of the Moai statues on Easter Island were made of tuff from the Rano Raraku volcano.

Argillite is similar to shale and slate. It is known for being dense and durable.

ARGILLITE

Argillite is a mudstone. When silt and clay mix with water, mud forms. The terms *silt* and *clay* are related to rock sizes. Silt is rock with an average grain size of between 0.00015 and 0.0025 inches (0.0039 and 0.0625 mm). Clay is rock with an average grain size of less than 0.00015 inches (0.0039 mm). When mud loses its moisture and hardens, it becomes mudstone. Argillite is made of mostly clay with some silt mixed into it.

ZEBRA STONE

Zebra stone is a type of argillite found in western Australia. The clay and silt particles in zebra stone consist mostly of quartz and white mica. The rock is white or light brown in color with brown stripes. It is often used for artwork such as ceramics or pottery. A type of black argillite can be found on Haida Gwaii, a group of islands off the western coast of Canada. The Haida people have long used this rock for carvings and sculptures.

ROCK SIZES

A solid mineral of any size can be a rock. The major rock size types, from smallest to largest, are clay, silt, sand, pebbles, cobbles, and boulders. Clay particles are smaller than 0.00015 inches (0.0039 mm) across. Boulders are larger than 10.1 inches (25.6 cm).

ARKOSE

Arkose is a type of sandstone. Sand grains range from 0.0025 to 0.079 inches (0.0625 to 2 mm) in size. Sand can be made up of many different rocks and minerals. Quartz is the most common mineral in sand. Arkose is composed mostly of quartz. But it contains at least 25 percent feldspar. Arkose can contain other minerals too. Usually, the rock forms as the result of a water current. The current carries and deposits feldspar-rich sand.

Some people believe the name arkose comes from the Greek word archaios, which means "ancient."

The Uluṟu monolith is located in Australia's Uluṟu-Kata Tjuṯa National Park. Because of the rock's spiritual significance, visitors are not allowed to climb it.

ULURU

One famous arkose rock is the Uluṟu monolith in western Australia. It is a large, reddish-colored rock formation that stands about 1,141 feet (348 m) tall. Today, the Uluṟu region of Australia is very dry. But about 900 to 600 million years ago, it was a sea. During that time, the sandstone that makes up Uluṟu formed. The monolith is known for its bright orange color at sunset. It is sacred to many Indigenous peoples in Australia.

Bauxite is known for its reddish-brown color and speckled, spotted appearance.

BAUXITE

Bauxite forms from residual soils rather than sediment. Residual soil comes from rock weathering. Whereas sediment is soil moved by wind or water, residual soil stays in the same place as the rock from which it came. Residual soil looks like loose rock or dirt covering a larger bedrock.

Bauxite commonly forms in tropical places. These parts of the world have wet and dry seasons. In these climates, plants grow on top of residual soil. The plants help dissolve some of the minerals in the rock.

ALUMINUM SOURCE

One mineral in bauxite is aluminum. This shiny gray

material is used in aluminum foil, cans, and other products. Aluminum does not dissolve easily. It remains even after other minerals have been carried away. When the soil that forms bauxite becomes rock, it is rich in aluminum. Today, bauxite is the world's biggest aluminum source. It is mined worldwide. Australia is the world's biggest producer of aluminum from bauxite.

BRECCIA

Breccia is the name for any sedimentary rock with large, sharp rock fragments. These fragments are at least 0.079 inches (2 mm) wide. This means that the different rock fragments inside breccia are visible.

Breccia is a clastic rock. This means it is formed from other rocks. Breccia forms when rocks are carried by water, ice, or wind. It can also form when rocks fall. These rocks are

Breccia rocks can form in a variety of ways, including through landslides and volcanic activity.

The West Elk Breccia in the US state of Colorado is composed of volcanic breccia.

joined together by finer-grained rocks or mineral cement. Mineral cement refers to the hardening of sediment in spaces between rocks. Cementation is the final step in the creation of a sedimentary rock. The fine-grained material in between crystals and clasts, or rock fragments, is also known as the rock matrix.

A MOTTLED ROCK

Breccia's varied rock fragments give it a mottled appearance. The fragments inside breccia may vary widely in color and shape. Breccia has been used for decorative purposes for thousands of years. In ancient Rome, breccia was considered a precious stone. It was commonly used in buildings and decorations.

Chalk is known for forming white cliffs along coastlines. One example is the Seven Sisters Cliffs in Sussex, United Kingdom.

CHALK

Chalk is a form of limestone. Like other limestones, it is made from calcium carbonate. This comes mostly from shells. These shells are often the fossils of microorganisms. Foraminifera, for instance, are single-celled sea organisms. They have existed for more than 500 million years. They have shells made of calcium carbonate. Ocean currents carry the shells of dead foraminifera

FOSSILS

Fossils are traces or remains of living things. Fossils can be left behind on rock, like footprints in sedimentary rock. Or they can be minerals themselves, such as bones, teeth, and shells. When these materials are inside a living being, they are not considered rocks. But after the organism's death, they can be considered rocks.

and other organisms as sediment. Deposits of this sediment become limestones such as chalk. They are often found on the ocean floor.

A SOFT, CRUSHABLE ROCK

Chalk is usually white or gray in color. It is porous, meaning it has many holes. Chalk is easy to crush and crumble. The chalk that artists use for drawing was once made from chalk rock mixed with clay. Today, drawing chalk is made of other materials. But the rock is still used to make putty. It is mixed in everyday products such as makeup and paint.

Natural chalk comes in limited colors and can be difficult to work with, so modern drawing chalks are usually made with pigments and special binding materials.

CLAYSTONE

Claystone is a type of mudstone with clay-sized particles. The properties of claystone depend on the type of clay it contains. For example, tonstein is a claystone that contains mostly the mineral kaolinite. Kaolinite is used to make ceramic materials such as china. It is also used as a coating for paper.

CLAYSTONE VS. CLAY

Tonstein is often too hard to be a good source of clay. Heat and pressure can indurate, or harden, sedimentary rocks. This process makes them much harder than the clay from which they formed. This is true even when the grains that make up the rock and the clay are the same size. Tonsteins are sometimes found as bands in other rocks. Bands of tonstein are common in coal deposits. These bands help scientists determine how old the deposits are.

Claystone has an earthy texture and is softer than many other types of rock. It comes in a range of colors, including red and orange.

The Painted Hills, which are located at Oregon's John Day Fossil Beds National Monument, feature colorful bands of claystone.

COAL

Coal is made of mostly organic material. Something that is organic comes from living things. On Earth, life-forms are carbon based. All living things, including plants and humans, contain carbon. When living things die, their remains return to the soil. Over time, the soil can become compacted. The carbon in dead plants turns into rock under pressure. It forms coal. While coal can contain other materials, it always consists of more than 50 percent carbon.

ENERGY SOURCE

Coal is a very powerful energy source. It is known as a fossil fuel because it comes from dead organisms. Burning coal creates steam that can be used to generate electricity. About 16 percent of the electricity in the United States comes from burning coal. However, when coal burns, it releases carbon into the atmosphere. This extra carbon traps heat inside the atmosphere, causing climate change. Burning coal is a major contributor to climate change around the world.

Coal helped fuel the Industrial Revolution of the 1800s. During this time, coal-powered factories began producing many goods.

Coal is often burned at power plants. Emissions from the coal are released into the air through the power plant's smokestacks.

CONGLOMERATE

Conglomerate is a clastic sedimentary rock. Like breccia, conglomerates contain rock fragments that are more than 0.079 inches (2 mm) wide. Rock fragments in conglomerate are rounded, while those in breccia are sharp.

Conglomerate can be made of many different types of rocks. It is defined by the way it forms rather than by its composition. This means conglomerates can look very different from one another.

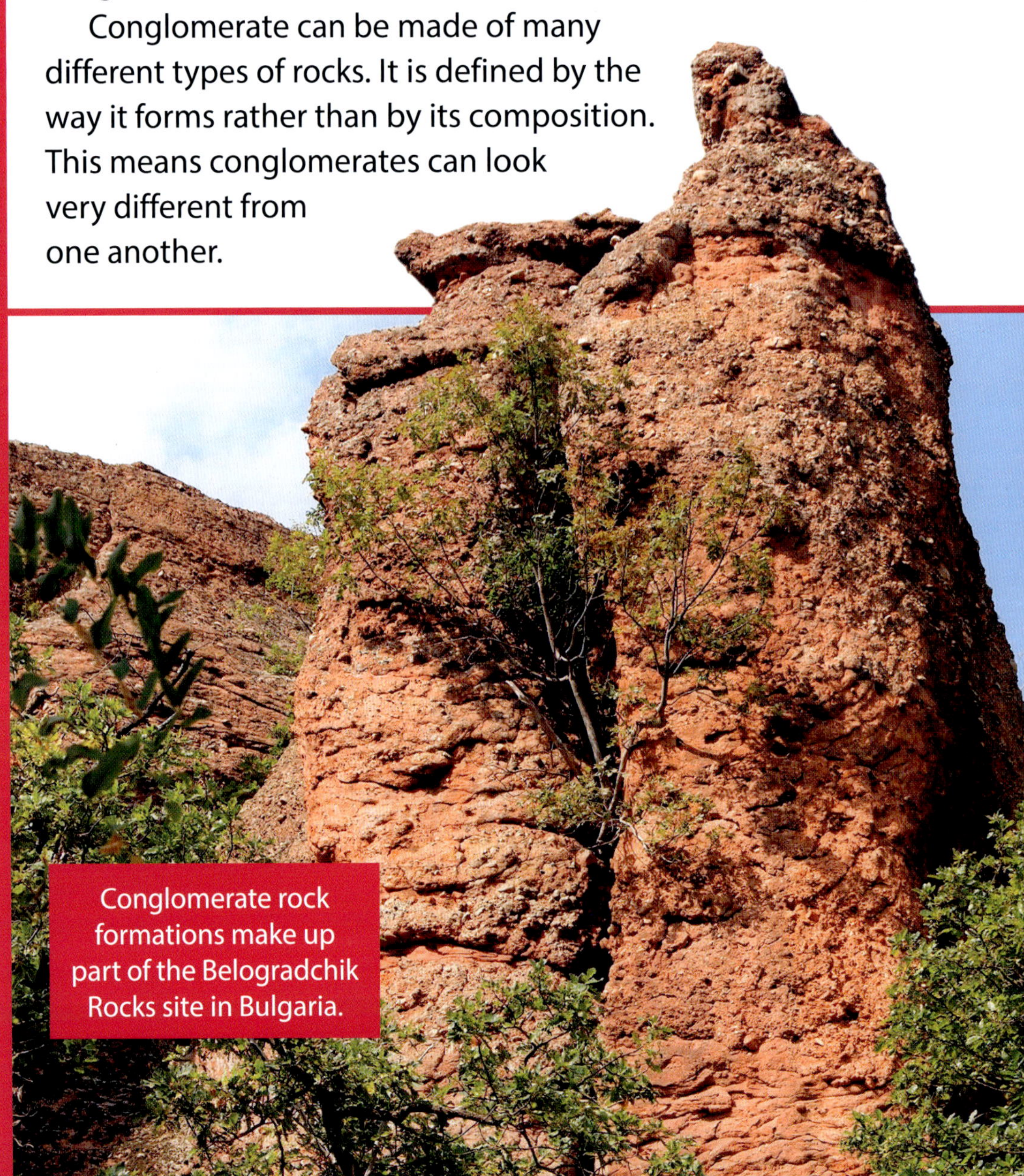

Conglomerate rock formations make up part of the Belogradchik Rocks site in Bulgaria.

CLUE TO EARTH'S EARLY HISTORY

Conglomerates usually form as a result of water currents. These can be freshwater or ocean currents. Because of this, conglomerates can be found worldwide. Some are extremely old.

In the 1980s, geologists began studying a conglomerate deposit in Jack Hills, Australia. They found crystals of the mineral zircon there. The zircon was more than four billion years old. Later, researchers found evidence that this zircon had formed alongside water. Back then, oceans and rivers were new on Earth. They were already setting the rock cycle in motion.

WHAT GEOLOGISTS DO

Geologists are scientists who study rocks. These rocks provide clues about Earth's history. There are many types of geologists. Marine geologists, for example, study the ocean floor. Other geologists study the chemical structures of rocks. Some help figure out where certain mineral deposits are located.

COQUINA

Most limestone is made of the shells of microscopic organisms. But larger sea creatures also have calcium carbonate shells. The shells of animals such as clams and oysters are made of calcium carbonate. Many corals have calcium carbonate skeletons too. Coquina is a limestone made of these larger shell fragments.

The shell pieces in coquina are visible. They are cemented together with smaller particles. But the shell fragments make up most of the rock. Because of this, coquina is very porous. It is sometimes called shell limestone. Coquina made of shells that are less than 0.079 inches (2 mm) wide is called microcoquina.

Coquina is usually found on beaches and shores. These are places where shells wash up

The name *coquina* is Spanish for "cockle." Cockles are a type of clamshell commonly found in coquina rocks.

and collect. Rainwater falls on the shells too. The acid in the rainwater dissolves some of the calcium carbonate. This helps the shells stick to one another and to the surrounding sand.

STURDY AND ABSORBENT

Coquina can be a very sturdy building material. Since it is porous, it can absorb shocks from things such as bullets and cannons. In the 1600s, a Spanish fort in Saint Augustine, Florida, was built with coquina. Its walls survived many enemy attacks.

Some diamictites form when glacial till, a mix of rock fragments moved by glaciers, solidifies. The resulting rocks are known as tillites.

DIAMICTITE

Diamictite is a clastic rock. It contains rock fragments of different sizes. It is also a type of mudstone. Diamictites are sometimes called conglomerate mudstones or pebbly mudstones.

DIAMICTITES AND GLACIER MOVEMENT

Diamictite can form in a few different ways. It often forms as a tillite rock. These rocks are created by glacial sediment. Icy glaciers form on land from precipitation such as snow. They are always in motion. The force of gravity causes the ice to flow slowly across the land. Because of this, glaciers are sometimes called "rivers of ice."

When a glacier moves, it reshapes the land. It picks up soil from the ground. The soil at the base of the glacier travels with it and is deposited in the glacier's path. This movement creates sedimentary rocks such as diamictites. Soil from the top of a glacier can be deposited by melting too. Other events, such as landslides, can also create diamictites. Scientists use these rocks to study the history of glaciers and their movements.

Diamictite is considered to be poorly sorted, meaning that it contains rock fragments and sediment grains that vary greatly in size.

Evaporite rocks can be found in the salt flats of the Cordillera de la Sal. This region is in Chile's Atacama Desert.

EVAPORITE

Evaporite is an example of a chemical sedimentary rock. The sediment forms from the chemical process of evaporation. This is the process by which something changes from a liquid into a vapor. Vapor particles are suspended in the air. Heat and pressure both cause evaporation. Water on Earth often contains dissolved minerals. When this water evaporates, the minerals are left behind. The resulting rocks are called evaporites.

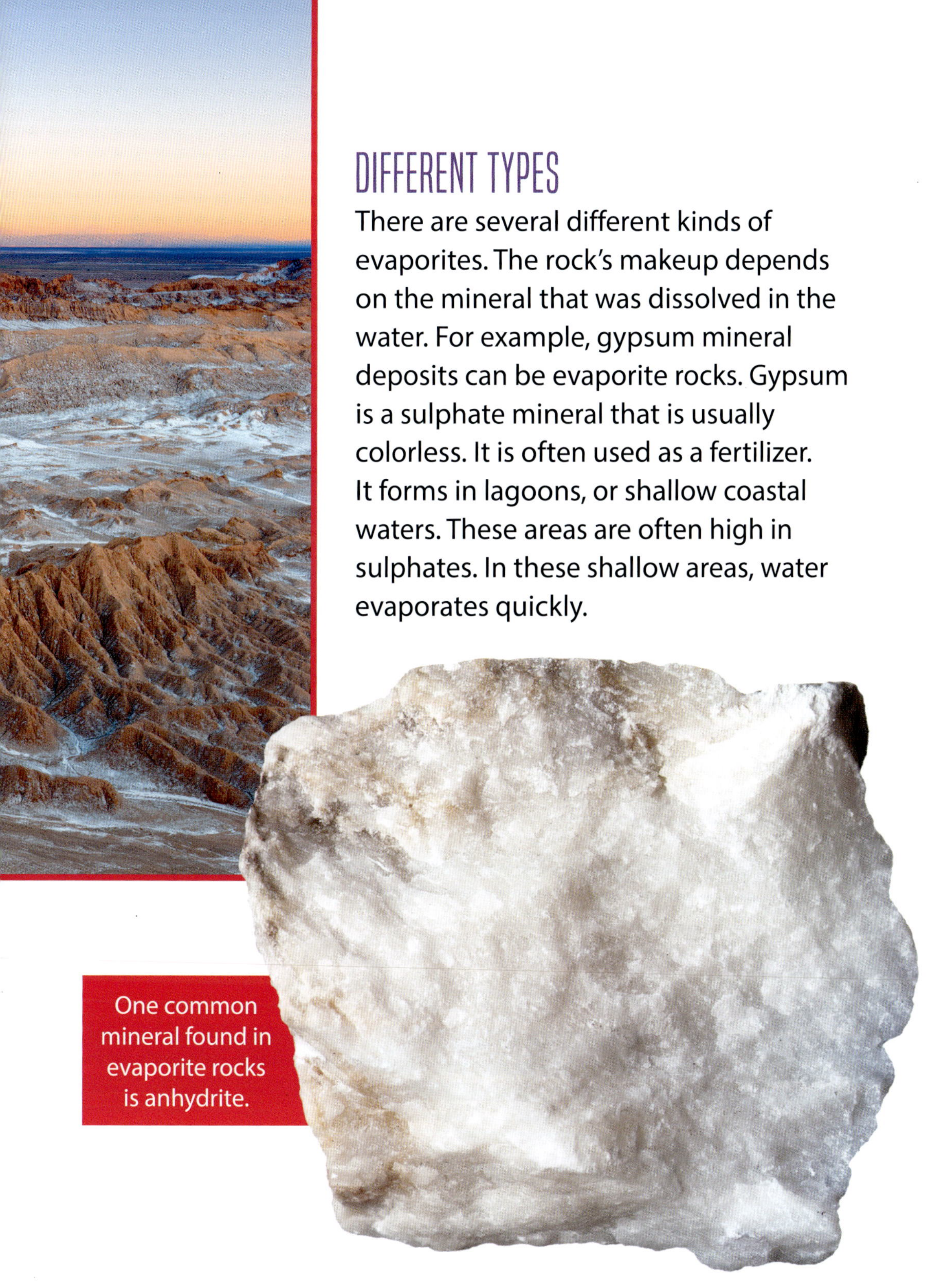

DIFFERENT TYPES

There are several different kinds of evaporites. The rock's makeup depends on the mineral that was dissolved in the water. For example, gypsum mineral deposits can be evaporite rocks. Gypsum is a sulphate mineral that is usually colorless. It is often used as a fertilizer. It forms in lagoons, or shallow coastal waters. These areas are often high in sulphates. In these shallow areas, water evaporates quickly.

One common mineral found in evaporite rocks is anhydrite.

FLINT

Flint is a type of chert, a silica-rich rock. It is dense, hard, and fine grained with few holes. Chert can form through several processes. It can be either a sedimentary or metamorphic rock. Flint is a sedimentary type of chert. It forms as nodes inside larger limestone deposits. This happens when hydrogen and oxygen mix inside the rock. They create an acidic environment. This dissolves the surrounding carbonate, forming silica.

AN EARLY STONE TOOL

Early humans used flint to make tools. The rock is both hard and brittle. Hard rocks do not crumble easily. But brittle rocks can be chipped and shaped. These qualities made flint a useful material for weapons. Early humans quarried flint and traded it across long distances. They formed some of the first trade routes in order to exchange the rock.

Flint has long been used as a fire-making tool. When the rock is struck against materials such as steel, it produces sparks.

Early humans
shaped flint into
arrowpoints,
axes, fishhooks,
and other tools.

Geyserite is usually light brown in color and has a lumpy appearance.

GEYSERITE

Geyserite is a chemical sedimentary rock. It is a sinter, or a lightweight rock made mostly of silica. It is also an evaporite. Geyserite is named after the geysers in which it often forms. Geysers are collections of groundwater, or water stored naturally underground, with vents that open onto Earth's surface. They are heated by pockets of nearby magma. The heat from the magma causes buildups of pressurized steam and gas. This causes a geyser to erupt hot water and steam, releasing the pressure. This process repeats as magma reheats and pressurizes the groundwater.

UNIQUE FORMATION

The water inside a geyser is surrounded by volcanic rock. Some of the silica inside this rock dissolves in the water. When a geyser erupts, the water it emits is very hot and evaporates quickly. The silica left behind from the evaporating water forms geyserite. At first, the silica from this evaporation forms into opal. Later, it becomes quartz. Opal and quartz are both made of silica. But opal has more water in it than quartz does. It also lacks a crystal structure.

Yellowstone National Park's Castle Geyser has a large cone around its opening. The cone consists of geyserite layers that built up over time.

GRAYWACKE

Wacke is a term for a sandstone containing 15 to 75 percent sand particles. This sandstone may also include clasts, or rock fragments, of other sizes. This means it is poorly sorted. Rocks that are poorly sorted have a wide variety of grain sizes, while well-sorted rocks have grains of the same size. The clasts in wacke can include many different rocks and minerals. In graywacke, they are made of quartz, feldspar, and other rocks.

HOW GRAYWACKE FORMS

Graywacke forms in the ocean from turbidity currents, sometimes called submarine avalanches. These are

Graywacke is often gray or black in color. It rates 6 to 7 on the Mohs scale.

giant, quick-moving, downward flows of water. They happen when water becomes heavy with sediment particles. These currents deposit sediment on the ocean floor. Turbidity currents create underwater canyons and can even cause tsunamis. Graywacke deposits are found in places where these currents flowed hundreds of millions of years ago.

Graywacke is commonly used in construction. Some seawalls are made of graywacke. These human-made barriers between the sea and land help prevent issues such as flooding.

JASPILITE

Jaspilite is a type of banded ironstone. Banded ironstones are very old rocks. They do not form in today's conditions. They come from what is called the Great Oxidation Event. This happened about 2.3 to 2.8 billion years ago. Before this, living things on Earth did not use oxygen. Then new life-forms called cyanobacteria evolved. These organisms were capable of a process called photosynthesis. This process released oxygen into the atmosphere, changing its makeup.

AN ANCIENT BANDED ROCK

Scientists believe that the oxygen in the atmosphere also changed the makeup of rocks. It created iron ores such as magnetite and hematite. These iron ores are present in jaspilite. They occur in bands, giving the rock a striped appearance. Jaspilite also contains jasper. Today, the rock can be found at Michigan's Jasper Knob. This site features a hill with exposed jaspilite. Visitors can view and touch the red and gray bands of rock. Today, higher oxygen levels in the atmosphere prevent iron from accumulating in oceans. This means banded ironstones cannot form.

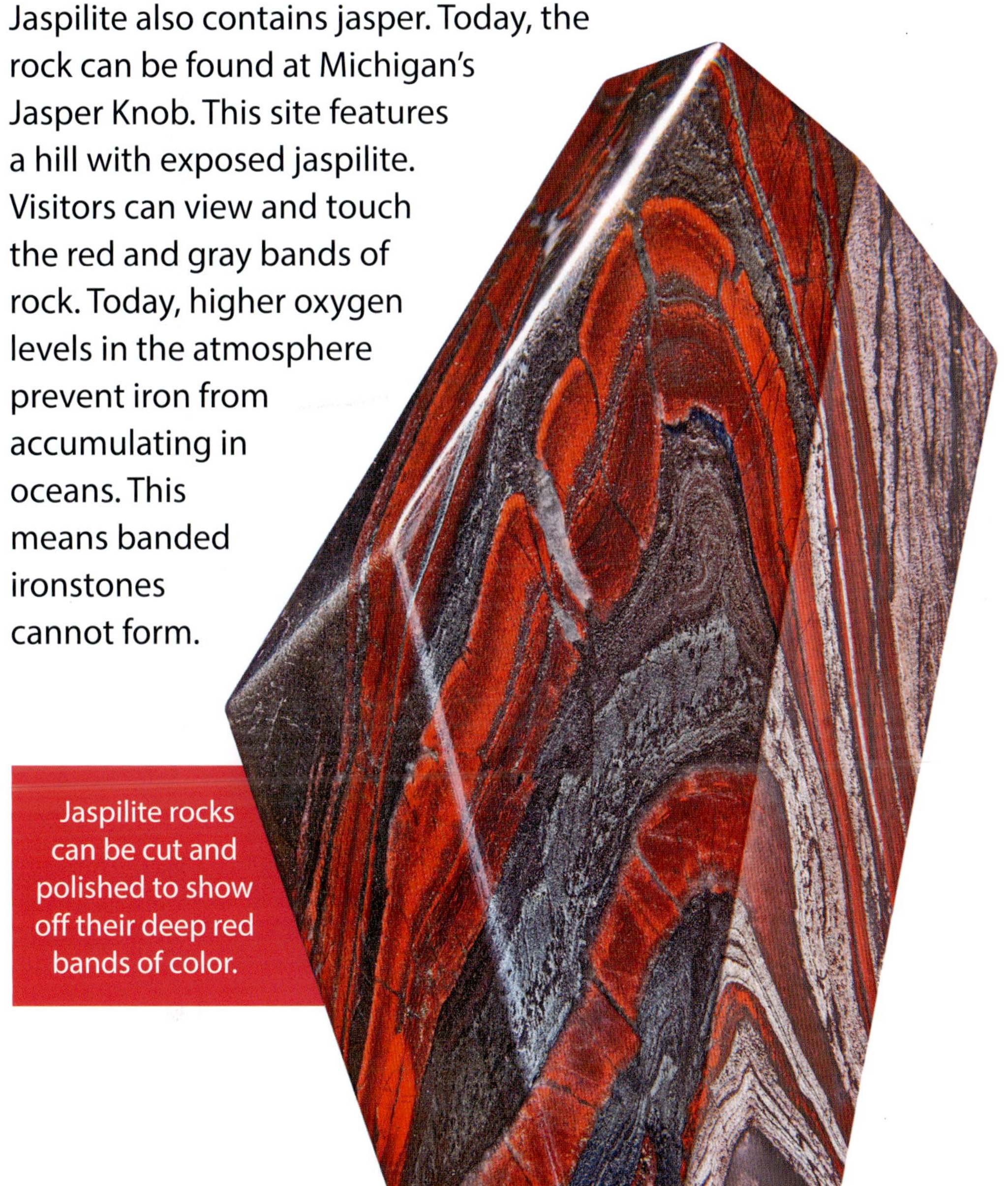

Jaspilite rocks can be cut and polished to show off their deep red bands of color.

LIMESTONE

Limestone is a common sedimentary rock. About 10 percent of Earth's sedimentary rocks are limestone. There are many types of limestone, including chalk, coquina, travertine, and tufa. A rock is a limestone if it consists mostly of the mineral calcium carbonate.

Limestone can be made of microorganisms such as foraminifera and cyanobacteria. It can also be made of the shells of life-forms such as clams and mussels. Limestone can form from other

GEODES AND THUNDER EGGS

Geodes and thunder eggs are rocks with empty spaces inside them. These spaces are partially filled with crystals. Geodes and thunder eggs both form in hollow spaces inside rocks. Geodes form inside sedimentary rocks such as limestone. Holes in a rock can form in several ways. For example, if an intact shell turns into limestone, a geode can form in the shell. Mineral water flows through the holes, depositing crystals over time. Thunder eggs form when there are holes in igneous rock. Trapped gases usually create these holes.

Limestone that has fossils embedded in it is called fossiliferous limestone.

limestones too. Existing limestone can be weathered or moved by natural forces. It can cement into new limestone rock.

LIMESTONE FORMATION, THEN AND NOW

Limestone can be as old as 2.8 billion years. But it is still forming today. For example, coral reefs create new limestone deposits. Limestone can also form in places where land meets water. Many islands, such as the Bahamas, are made of limestone rock. The White Cliffs of Dover on the coast of England are a famous example of a limestone deposit. The cliffs showcase the rock's light color. The erosion that created the cliffs is partly due to the softness of the limestone.

Marlstone consists of lithified, or hardened, marl.

MARLSTONE

Marlstone is a rock made of silt and clay combined with calcium carbonate. The term *marl* describes a mixture of clay, silt, and calcium carbonate that has not cemented into rock. Marlstone is often described as a combination of mudstone and limestone.

A SOIL FERTILIZER

Marlstone is usually white or gray in color. It can form in seawater or fresh water. The rock is sometimes used as a soil fertilizer. Many rocks that contain calcium carbonate are used for this purpose. This is because calcium carbonate dissolves in acid. Acidic soils can be toxic to plants. They affect which nutrients and toxins reach the plants. Adding calcium carbonate to soil reduces the soil's acidity. However, rocks with high levels of calcium carbonate do not always produce good soil. Soil with a lot of calcium carbonate can measure too high on the pH scale for plants to thrive. This means farmers must carefully balance what they add to their soils.

In 1953, marl fertilizer was
used to prepare turf for
a cricket match between
England and Australia.
The match took place in
London, England.

MICROBIALITE

Microbialites are sedimentary rocks that have organic origins. These rocks come from communities of microbes at the bottom of a body of water. Microbes are single-celled, simple organisms such as bacteria and algae. They are usually too small to be seen with the naked eye.

FORMING MICROBIALITES

Communities of microbes can trap and bind surrounding sediment. They can also deposit solids such as limestone from their bodies. One type of microbialite is stromatolite. It is formed by both processes.

Cyanobacteria produce calcium carbonate. This creates limestone. Communities of cyanobacteria also trap layers

Thrombolites are a type of round microbialite. Visitors can see these formations at Lake Clifton in western Australia.

Living stromatolites in Hamelin Pool, located in Australia's Shark Bay, date back 3.5 billion years.

of sediment. Together, these sediment and limestone layers form stromatolites.

Some fossil stromatolites are hundreds of millions of years old. They can be found in the US state of Utah, the Indian Ocean, and other places. There are also formations known as living stromatolites in places such as the Australian coast. These stromatolites still have cyanobacteria living on them.

PLASTIGLOMERATES

Conglomerates form when bigger rock fragments are cemented by smaller grains of sediment. But humans have introduced a new cement into Earth's ecosystem: plastic. Plastic is a human-made product that can be easily bent, shaped, and molded. The material can have many sources, such as plant fiber, coal, and oil. Plastic melts at somewhat low temperatures. But it does not break down easily. About 22 million short tons (20 million metric tons) of plastic enter the environment each year. This can happen when people litter or flush plastic waste. It can also happen when garbage is dumped outside or in rivers.

Melted plastic can mix with and bind surrounding sediment. The resulting rocks are called plastiglomerates. Plastiglomerates can also form when melted plastic attaches to existing rocks.

IN SITU PLASTIGLOMERATES

Plastic can flow into cracks inside and between rocks. These are called in situ plastiglomerates. The phrase *in situ* means "in the original place." These rocks form on beaches, at campsites, and in other places where people discard plastic. In situ plastiglomerates can also be moved from place to place through processes such as weathering.

ROCK SALT

Rock salt is a common type of evaporite. It is made of halite, or salt. A molecule of salt consists of one sodium atom and one chlorine atom bonded together. The mineral structure of salt can take many forms but is often cubic. This is why salt flakes tend to look like small cubes.

The salt in the ocean comes from rocks. Rainwater on land weathers the minerals in rocks. These minerals end up in the ocean. Underwater volcanic eruptions and heat from magma can increase the salt content of oceans too. In the ocean, this salt stays dissolved in the water. When seawater reaches a

One variety of rock salt is pink Himalayan salt, which comes from the Punjab region of Pakistan.

shallow basin, this changes. The ocean water evaporates, and the salt stays behind. As this process continues, rock salt forms.

ON TABLES AND ROADS

Today, most rock salt comes from underground. It is the result of salt deposits formed by ancient water basins. This salt is mined for use as a food seasoning and preservative. It is also used as a deicing salt on icy roads in the winter.

SANDSTONE

Any sedimentary rock made from sand is known as sandstone. Most sandstones are more than 80 to 90 percent quartz. This is partly because granite, the most common rock on Earth's surface, is rich in quartz. The weathering of granite produces much of the world's sand.

Sandstone is the second-most-common type of sedimentary rock after shale.

BANDS AND LAYERS

Many sandstones have a banded formation. There are horizontal layers of different colors in the rock. This is because sandstone forms in layers over time. Older layers sit at the bottom, while newer layers sit above them. Geologists can analyze these rock layers to find clues about Earth's geological history.

Not all banded sandstone features horizontal layers. Sometimes, tectonic plate movement pushes bands of sandstone upward. The resulting sandstone is folded and squashed into peaks. Parts of the Appalachian Mountains are examples of these folded sandstone formations.

Arizona's Antelope Canyon is famous for its banded sandstone walls. Visitors can take tours of the site.

ANTELOPE CANYON

- Arizona's Antelope Canyon has a wave-like structure that gives it a unique look and, along with the canyon's glorious light beams, makes it the most photographed slot canyon in the southwestern United States. Slot canyons are very narrow canyons.
- Antelope Canyon is part of the Navajo Sandstone, a sedimentary rock formation. Wind and water caused deposits of sand to build up over time, forming the canyon's colorful layers.
- The canyon's unique geography was created by water that rushed along its walls over many, many years.
- Upper Antelope Canyon is at around 4,000 feet (1,200 m) in elevation.

The canyon's sandstone walls rise 120 feet (37 m) above the streambed.
Antelope Canyon is renowned worldwide for its flowing red rock formations, making it a popular destination for nature enthusiasts.

SEPTARIA

Septaria are sometimes called fossilized mud bubbles. They are concretions, or hardened circular rocks found inside sediment or sedimentary rocks. Concretions form when things such as pebbles or leaves get stuck in sediment. Before the sediment turns into rock, it contains water with dissolved minerals in it. These minerals precipitate. A dissolved mineral precipitates when it leaves the water and crystallizes. In this case, the mineral crystallizes around a pebble or leaf. This creates a hard, bubble-shaped mass that cements more quickly than the rest of the rock. These concretions appear round on the outside.

STRANGE AND BEAUTIFUL

Septarian concretions feature what looks like a crack in the middle, with crystals expanding outward. These rocks are

Septaria get their name from the Latin word *septum*, which means "boundary" or "partition."

sometimes called beetle stones because their crystal pattern resembles a beetle's body. Septaria can contain crystals of all types and colors. The rocks are admired for their beauty. Some people believe they have spiritual properties. The rocks are believed to bring a sense of grounding and calm.

Septaria are sometimes called septarian nodules or dragon stones. Some contain crystals inside their cracks.

DID YOU KNOW?

The Klerksdorp spheres are famous concretions found in South Africa. These rocks are so perfectly round that some people believe they were left behind by aliens from outer space.

Shale easily breaks apart. It rates between 1 and 4 on the Mohs scale.

SHALE

Shale is the most common sedimentary rock on Earth. About 70 percent of the sedimentary rocks on Earth's crust are shale. This fine-grained mudstone is known for its fissility, or ability to split into sheets. Shale is a laminated rock. This means it forms from layered deposits of mud, silt, and clay. In rock form, shale has thin layers that are easy to break apart. Shale layers can be combined with layers of sandstone or limestone. Like sandstone, shale is rich in quartz. Some fossil fuels, such as oil, can also be found in shale.

OIL SHALES

Mud often contains organic matter such as microorganisms and decomposing plants. Shales that contain this type of organic matter are known as oil shales. These shales tend to be dark in color. Oil shale is a source of oil and natural gas. There are also liquid deposits of oil between the cracks of oil shale deposits. This is called tight oil. It is released from shale deposits through a process called fracking. During fracking, workers inject liquid into rock to break it apart. This process can pollute water sources and cause earthquakes.

SILCRETE

Silcrete is a type of conglomerate. It consists of sand and gravel cemented by silica. Silcrete forms at the top of Earth's crust, where soil turns into rock. Silcrete is a hard rock that does not weather easily. Because it resists weathering, silcrete boulders can be quite large. Some can be seen at Stonehenge, an ancient stone monument built in England about 5,000 years ago. The largest stones at Stonehenge are silcrete boulders placed by humans.

Silcrete is a duricrust, or a hard rock that forms at or near Earth's surface.

A TECHNOLOGICAL BREAKTHROUGH

Early humans living in southern Africa and Australia used silcrete to make tools. Some of these tools are hundreds of thousands of years old. Early humans discovered that they could heat silcrete to keep it from flaking. This helped them make stronger tools out of the rock.

Taconite is often processed into small pellets that contain about 65 percent iron.

TACONITE

Like jaspilite, taconite is a type of banded iron formation. It is also known as banded-ferruginous chert. Something that is ferruginous contains iron. Like other cherts, taconite is a hard, fine-grained, and dense rock. It contains about 20 to 30 percent magnetite, which is an iron ore. Magnetite is known for its strong magnetic properties. People first discovered magnetism through a type of magnetite called lodestone. It can attract other magnetic metals. It was used to make the first compasses.

AN ORE OF STEEL

Today, most magnetite is used as an ore of steel. Steel is the most important metal in manufacturing, large-scale building, and industry. Taconite is a prime source of magnetite for steel. The United States is the world's largest producer of magnetite from taconite. The states of Minnesota and Michigan both contain large taconite deposits.

Taconite processing is a major industry along Minnesota's North Shore. The rock is processed in the town of Silver Bay.

TILL

Till is a general term for sedimentary rock formed by glaciers. As glaciers move, they collect and deposit sediment. Glacial movement has shaped much of Earth's land. Today, glaciers cover land in North America, South America, Greenland, northern Europe, central Asia, and Antarctica. As recently as 20,000 years ago, 25 percent of the land on Earth was covered in glaciers.

Glaciers erode rocks and soil as they move. They create landforms such as valleys and moraines. Moraines are buildups of rock and soil left behind by a glacier. They form under,

The rock fragments in till come in many shapes and sizes. Very tiny particles of till are known as glacial flour.

above, and beside glaciers as they move. Moraines are clues to a glacier's path across the land. They are found on every continent on Earth.

EROSION AND GEOLOGICAL HISTORY

The till in a moraine tells a glacier's story. The particles in till erode as they travel with a glacier. The longer these particles travel, the more they erode. This means the smaller fragments in till usually traveled longer than the bigger ones.

There are two types of till. Basal till forms at the bottom of a glacier, while ablation till forms at the top. Both types of till are useful to scientists. Researchers can study till to re-create the paths of glaciers and study Earth's geological history.

At Mammoth Hot Springs in Yellowstone National Park, visitors can see a series of colorful travertine terraces.

TRAVERTINE

Travertine is a form of limestone. Unlike most limestone, travertine forms from fresh water. It deposits in layers from springs. Most travertine comes from hot springs. The hot water in these springs speeds up the process of evaporation and rock formation.

Travertine is still being formed today. It is present in Yellowstone National Park, which is located in the states of Wyoming, Montana, and Idaho. The hot springs in the park deposit about 0.12 inches (3 mm) of travertine each day. This is partly because bacteria inside the hot springs help create calcium carbonate.

STALAGMITES AND STALACTITES

Travertine can also form in limestone caves. Water flows through these caves, leaving calcium carbonate behind. Travertine can accumulate in stalactites and stalagmites. Stalactites hang downward from a cave's ceiling. Stalagmites rise upward from the cave's floor. Both tend to have spiky shapes. Their shape reflects the flow of water through the cave. Minerals precipitate, or collect as solids, from this water flow.

New Mexico's Carlsbad Caverns feature many travertine stalactites and stalagmites.

TUFA

Tufa is a type of limestone. It is a chemical sedimentary rock. Like travertine, tufa precipitates out of water. The calcium carbonate dissolved in the water is left behind when the water evaporates. The resulting rock is soft and porous. In this way, it differs from travertine, which is a harder, denser limestone.

TUFA FORMATION

Tufa is still forming near Yosemite National Park in California. The area's Mono Lake contains alkaline water. When this lake water combines with water from springs, tufa

Tufa can form in a variety of places, including hot springs, rivers, and caves.

towers form. These are spiky tufa deposits. Tufa's porous texture gives it a rough, jagged look.

The rock is sometimes used for building and construction purposes. Tufa is used to make flowerpots too. The calcium carbonate in the rock enriches the pot's soil.

AMPHIBOLITE

Amphibolite is a hard, heavy metamorphic rock. It is made of plagioclase and a mineral called amphibole. Metamorphic rocks form when an existing rock undergoes a change. The original rock from which the metamorphic rock forms is called its protolith. Amphibolite can have many different protoliths. These can include igneous rocks and sedimentary rocks. Today, amphibolite is often used to make highways and railroads.

Rocks can metamorphose in several different ways. The most common way is through heat and pressure. Both heat and pressure change the movement of molecules in the rock. This can change the rock's crystal structure. These changes are different from the melting that turns rocks into magma. In metamorphic processes, the rock stays solid as it changes structure.

Amphibolite is coarse grained and comes mainly in black, green, and brown colors.

Amphibolite from New York's Adirondack Mountains is known for containing large garnets. These deep red gemstones are considered valuable.

GRADES OF METAMORPHISM

Low-grade metamorphism is the term for metamorphism that occurs under low heat and pressure. High-grade metamorphism is metamorphism that occurs under high heat and pressure. Metamorphism can happen between these grades. Amphibolite is a high-grade metamorphic rock.

The Latin or Greek word *lith* means "rock." In English, many scientific and historical words have Latin or Greek roots. That's why so many geology words have *lith* in them.

ANTHRACITE

Anthracite is metamorphosed coal. It forms when coal is exposed to high temperatures and pressures. Sedimentary coal has more than 50 percent carbon. But anthracite contains at least 86 percent. The rock is dark, hard, and shiny. Unlike softer coals, anthracite is clean to the touch. It does not smudge.

FUEL SOURCE

Anthracite was once used to heat homes. Some people still heat their homes with anthracite. But the rock is less common than sedimentary coal. Today, sedimentary coal is a more popular fuel.

Anthracite is hard and brittle. Unlike other forms of coal, it has a metallic luster.

Anthracite is not the only form of metamorphosed coal. Higher temperatures and pressures can produce other types. For example, meta-anthracite is metamorphosed anthracite. It contains at least 98 percent carbon. Like coal and anthracites, diamonds form from carbon. But diamonds are not metamorphosed coal. They come from crystallized carbon in other rocks.

Oregon's Coquille River Jetty, located at the mouth of the Coquille River, is made of blueschist rocks.

BLUESCHIST

A schist is a type of metamorphic rock. Schists are foliated, or made of thin mineral sheets. The rocks form through dynamic metamorphism. This occurs in places where rocks move against one another, such as at tectonic plate boundaries.

Movement between rocks at these boundaries can break, bend, and crush the rock. These movements put strong

pressure on underground rock. This pressure creates the layered sheets found in schists. Blueschist forms in subduction zones. These are places where one tectonic plate goes underneath another.

BLUE COLOR

Blueschists often have a blue color, which comes from alkali crystals. These are compounds formed by alkali metals. The rock is similar to another type of schist called greenschist. But the two schists have different colors and grades of metamorphism. Greenschists form under slightly lower pressure than blueschists.

CATACLASITE

Cataclasite is a type of fault rock. These are rocks that form in faults, or fractures between rocks. In faults, rocks may pull apart. They may touch or grind together. Faults can be very short or very long. The longest fault in the world is the San Andreas Fault, which is 745 miles (1,200 km) long. It runs down the western side of California.

The San Andreas Fault runs through California's Carrizo Plain. Cataclasite rocks have been found in and around the fault.

DYNAMIC METAMORPHISM

Cataclasite forms from dynamic metamorphism in faults. At a fault, rocks are crushed or cracked apart by friction and pressure. They re-form inside a crushed rock matrix. This is the finer-grained mass that surrounds the clasts, or rock fragments. Cataclasites contain about 50 to 90 percent matrix. This matrix can sometimes appear glassy. This happens when friction and stress cause the rock to partially melt.

ECLOGITE

Eclogite is a high-grade metamorphic rock. More than 75 percent of it consists of a combination of garnet and a pyroxene called omphacite. Eclogite is chemically similar to basalt. Basalt is often its protolith. Like greenschist and blueschist, eclogite forms in subduction zones. But it forms under higher pressures and temperatures. This means that eclogite typically originates farther underground. There, rock is under more pressure than rock at the surface.

Eclogite is green with red or pink spots. The green color comes from omphacite, while the reddish color comes from garnet.

A POSSIBLE MANTLE ROCK

Some geologists believe there is a lot of eclogite in Earth's upper mantle. However, the mantle is difficult to study. To reach it, geologists must drill very deep holes. The mantle is hot enough to destroy most equipment. The first successful drilling of Earth's mantle occurred in 2023. Geologists found peridotite samples. Peridotites, like eclogite, are rich in the mineral olivine.

Eclogite is often tumbled
and polished to show off
its unique pattern.

FRUCHTSCHIEFER

Fruchtschiefer is a type of slate. Slate is typically metamorphosed shale. It is a low-grade metamorphic rock. It may retain some features of its protolith, such as rock layers. Fruchtschiefer's protolith is argillite.

Fruchtschiefer is a spotted slate. It contains porphyroblasts. These are similar to phenocrysts in igneous rocks. Porphyroblasts form as chunks of single crystals. They are created throughout the metamorphic process. Pressure, heat, and stress cause rocks to recrystallize. Sometimes, a large grain of a new crystal type emerges. This crystal stays within the larger rock matrix.

Fruchtschiefer is one of several types of spotted slate, or slate with spots or flecks in it.

A GERMAN ROCK

Fruchtschiefer was first found in Germany. Its name comes from the German words for "fruit" or "grain" and "slate" or "schist." The rock got its name because its grains look like wheat grains. Today, the rock is used in sculptures and as a building material.

Fulgurite is often described as petrified or fossilized lightning. The rock's name comes from the Latin word *fulgur*, meaning "lightning."

FULGURITE

Fulgurite is a type of pyrometamorphic rock. These are rocks that metamorphose quickly because of heat. Pyrometamorphic rocks are different from high-grade and low-grade metamorphic rocks. High- and low-grade rocks metamorphose from a combination of heat and pressure. For pyrometamorphic rocks, heat is the main factor.

In the case of fulgurite, the heat comes from lightning. Fulgurite is a silica-rich glass. It forms when lightning strikes and melts sand or other rock. The heat from the lightning quickly melts the sand, which rapidly cools.

TUBES OF LIGHTNING

Sand fulgurites tend to look like branching tubes. Their shape follows the path of lightning as it hits Earth. They tend to be small in diameter but can be up to 66 feet (20 m) long. Rock fulgurites look like glass coatings on existing rocks. These fulgurites are often found on mountaintops. This is because high elevations such as mountain peaks attract more lightning than lower elevations.

When lightning strikes a surface, it often fans out in multiple directions. This can form fulgurites with many twisting, hollow tubes that look like tree branches or roots.

GNEISS

Like schist, gneiss is a medium-grade to high-grade metamorphic rock that features layered bands. But schist differs from gneiss in that it is easy to break apart in parallel layers. Gneiss is not easy to split in this way. This is because less than half the minerals in gneiss are in parallel layers. When minerals are not lined up in parallel layers, they are harder to break apart.

AMONG THE OLDEST ROCKS

There are many types of gneiss, and each has a different mineral makeup. Common protoliths of gneiss include granite and shale. Some of the world's oldest rocks

Gneiss often features a pattern of alternating dark-colored and light-colored bands. This is known as gneissic banding.

are gneiss. The Acasta gneisses are gneiss deposits located in northwestern Canada. They have been part of Earth's crust for about four billion years. This means they are older than life on Earth. But these gneisses are not the oldest rocks to exist. They are metamorphic rocks, so they had even older protoliths.

HORNFELS

Hornfels is a type of granofels. Granofels is a rock that is not usually foliated, or made of thin mineral sheets. This makes the rocks different from other metamorphic rocks, such as schist. Granofels form from contact metamorphism. This happens when heat from nearby magma changes existing rocks.

Hornfels is a fine-grained rock. Unlike schist, the crystals in hornfels are not arranged in parallel rows. The rock can consist of many different minerals. It comes in a wide range of colors too. Its protoliths can be igneous, sedimentary, or metamorphic.

TOUGH AND HORN-LIKE

The name *hornfels* comes from a German word meaning "horn rock." The rock's toughness and shape reminded miners of animal horns. In England, hornfels was sometimes called whetstone. Today, the rock is used in construction as a flooring material.

In 1840, a British musician used hornfels stones from Cumbria, England, to make a lithophone instrument. Today, these rocks are known as the Skiddaw Stones.

One type of impactite is tagamite. This impact melt rock was first discovered in the Popigai crater in Siberia.

IMPACTITE

Impactite forms from a special type of contact metamorphism. It is a result of the contact or collision of planets or space objects. When large meteorites hit Earth, they do so with great force. The impact heats and pressurizes rock.

MOLDAVITE

One type of impactite is called moldavite. It is the result of a meteorite that landed in what is now Germany about 15 million years ago. The meteorite liquified silica rock, sending it flying. This resulted in fields strewn with a green, silica-rich glass. People in the area traded and carved this moldavite. The Venus of Willendorf is a figure of a woman that was carved from limestone about 25,000 years ago. When the figure was found, fragments of moldavite were discovered alongside it. This suggests that people living at the time prized this rare rock.

Moldavite is a type
of tektite, or impact
glass. It is known
for its unique
shape and bumpy,
pitted surface.

JADE

Two high-grade metamorphic rocks are commonly called jade. These are jadeite and nephrite. Jadeite consists of a mineral called jadeite pyroxene. Nephrite is made of actinolite and tremolite crystals. Both rocks are hard and heavy. They come in many colors, but green is the most prized.

A PRIZED ROCK

People have used jade for thousands of years. The rock came into wide use during the Neolithic Period, which began about 12,000 years ago. During this time, people used a variety of stone tools.

Jade also has a long history in Chinese culture. The stone is considered extremely valuable. It is associated with virtues such as warmth, purity, and bravery. Jade has been used in Chinese jewelry, decoration, and pottery for more than 5,000 years.

Jadeite and nephrite, *pictured*, look similar but consist of different minerals. Nephrite also tends to be less translucent than jadeite.

DID YOU KNOW?

Just as fossils are remains from nature, old pieces of pottery are rock remains from past cultures. Archaeologists study ancient pottery to learn how people lived and how trade networks functioned.

In ancient China, jade was prized for its durability and luster. Artisans carved jade into intricate statues, jewelry, and religious items.

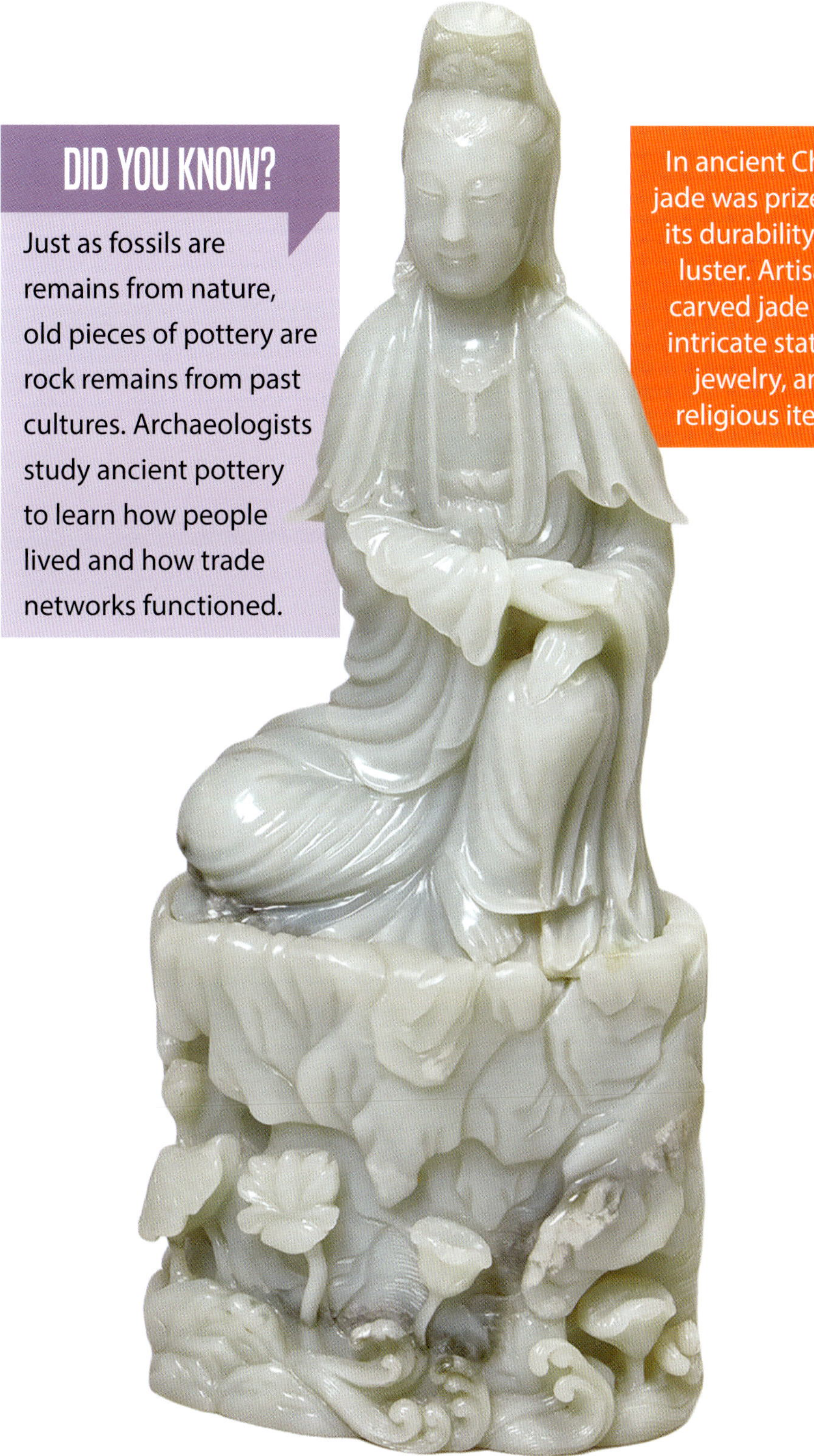

LAPIS LAZULI

Lapis lazuli is a meta-evaporite. This means its protolith is an evaporite. It is a high-grade metamorphic rock. Its primary material is lazurite, a bright blue mineral. However, the rock contains other minerals too. Lapis lazuli gems are made from the whole rock, not just the lazurite. The rock also contains small, golden grains of pyrite, a mineral known as "fool's gold."

BRILLIANT BLUES

Lapis lazuli is valued for its striking blue color. The rock's name comes from the Persian word *lazawad*. The English word *azure*, along with the Italian and Spanish words for "blue," come from this word. Afghanistan is the primary source of lapis lazuli. The rock has been mined for thousands of years. Ancient Sumerian and Egyptian royalty wore jewelry made from the rock.

The funeral mask of King Tutankhamen, an ancient Egyptian pharaoh, is inlaid with lapis lazuli. The rock is featured on the eyes and eyebrows of the mask.

LISTVENITE

Listvenite is sometimes called listwanite or listwaenite. It is a metasomatic rock. This type of rock changes form through chemical reactions. Listvenite forms when peridotite is exposed to water that contains a lot of carbon. The carbon in the water changes the rock's makeup.

Listvenite often has a bright green color. This hue comes from a mineral called fuchsite. The color also forms from a reaction with carbon. Listvenite is widely distributed. There are listvenite deposits on every continent except Australia and Antarctica.

Listvenite contains minerals such as quartz, dolomite, and magnesite.

A CARBON SINK

Listvenite captures carbon. The carbon inside the rock is locked inside stable minerals. These minerals contain carbon but don't break down easily. Carbon that enters listvenite tends to stay there. Today, geologists are looking for ways to remove extra carbon from the atmosphere. Rocks such as listvenite could be one solution.

MARBLE

Marble is metamorphosed limestone. It is not a hard rock, but it is harder than its protolith. Pure marble has a white color. It can be polished to a high shine. Other marbles come in colors such as pink or black. Limestone can contain minerals and impurities such as silt and clay. When limestone changes into marble, these materials form swirls in the rock.

STATUES AND SURFACES

Marble's color, softness, and shine make it ideal for statues. The Italian sculptor Michelangelo carved his famous sculpture of David from a single block of marble. Marble is commonly used as a building material. It is found in buildings and on indoor surfaces such as counters and tabletops. Marble breaks easily, so it must be carefully quarried and mined. About half of all quarried marble shatters and goes to waste.

Michelangelo's *David* is sculpted from white Carrara marble quarried in Carrara, Italy. This popular type of marble has been used for many buildings and statues.

METAPELITE

Metapelite is also called pelitic rock or metamudstone. *Pelite* is another word for mudstone. Metapelite is metamorphosed mudstone. These rocks can metamorphose in a few different ways. Their protoliths can become part of mountains. The rock inside the mountain can then metamorphose under heat and pressure. Mudstones can also metamorphose from the heat of nearby magma. They can be pressurized after being pushed underground when tectonic plates collide.

Common minerals found in metapelites include staurolite and kyanite.

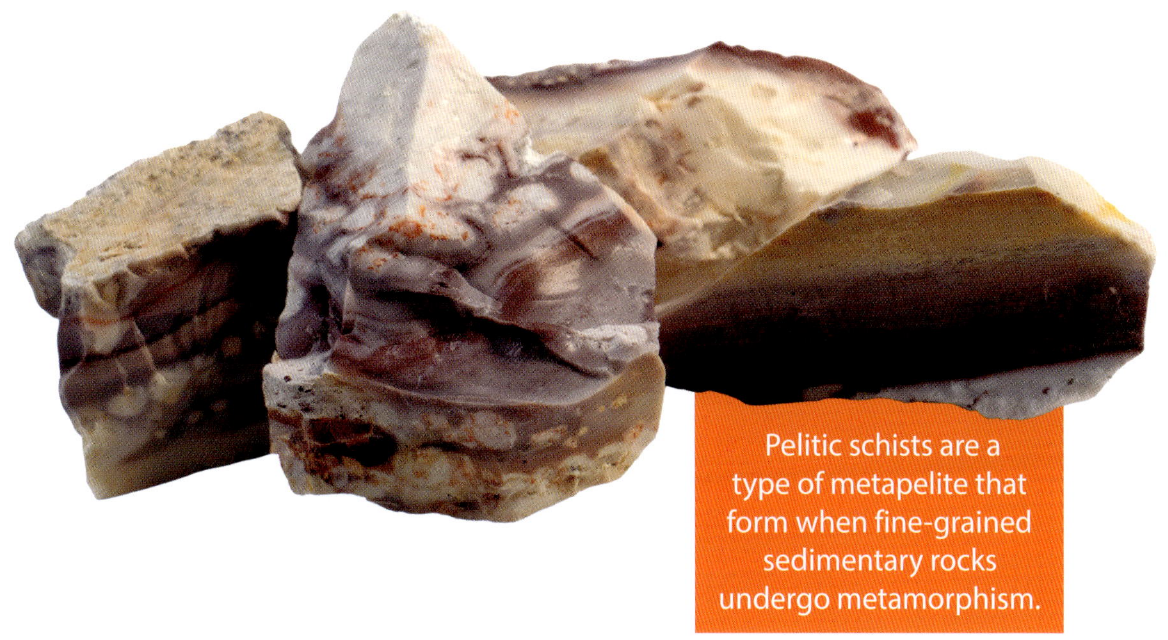

METAMORPHISM AND CRYSTAL TYPES

The grade of a rock's metamorphosis helps determine which crystals form in it. When any type of rock undergoes low-grade metamorphism, minerals such as chlorite and muscovite form. High-grade metamorphism can form minerals such as kyanite and sillimanite. Metapelites can be low, medium, or high grade.

These grades of metamorphism were discovered by Scottish geologist George Barrow. In 1912, Barrow discovered that mudstones metamorphosed on a scale, from low heat and pressure to high heat and pressure. Rocks near the surface are less heated and pressurized than rocks deep underground. As a result, they recrystallize differently. Sometimes, related rocks that have experienced different amounts of heat and pressure are found near one another. This is called regional metamorphism.

MIGMATITE

Migmatite is a banded rock with varied layers. This high-grade metamorphic rock is mixed with streaks or veins of granite. These streaks form when parts of the rock melt during metamorphosis. The melted parts become magma and cool into igneous rock. The rest of the rock metamorphoses but stays solid. In this way, migmatite is like a cross between an igneous and a metamorphic rock.

GEOLOGICAL RESEARCH

Migmatites form at tectonic boundaries. They can be created when a mountain or mountain range emerges. They offer clues about Earth's geological history. Geologists can use migmatites to trace the past boundaries of tectonic plates.

Migmatites also play a role in hydrogeology. This is the study of water in Earth's crust. Studying migmatites can help people assess the quality of nearby groundwater, or water stored naturally underground. Water absorbs minerals from nearby rock, so the minerals in migmatites may affect the quality of nearby water.

Migmatites feature light-colored bands called leucosomes and dark-colored bands called melanosomes.

MYLONITE

Mylonite is a fault rock and a type of cataclasite. It forms in shear zones. These are places where rocks are under stress from rubbing against one another. The rocks break apart into fine grains. Then they recrystallize and come back together.

Mylonite can have larger rock fragments inside it. It can have many protoliths too. Mylonites with quartz or feldspar protoliths are called phyllonites.

Mylonite rocks are fine grained and often feature streaks or bands.

ROAD AGGREGATE

Mylonite is often used as a part of road aggregate. It is mined, crushed, and added to the rock mix used to make roads. These mixes can be natural, human-made, or recycled from other aggregates. Rocks used for road aggregate are chosen carefully. They must be hard enough to resist erosion. They must be durable and strong. They must also allow water to drain so that roads don't become waterlogged.

PHYLLITE

Phyllite is similar to slate. It is dark in color. The rock's main material is quartz. Quartz crystals, like other crystals, come in various sizes. In phyllite, the quartz crystals are quite small. Unlike slate, phyllite does not contain clay minerals. Phyllite also goes through a slightly higher-grade metamorphism than slate does.

CLEAVAGE PLANES

Phyllite consists of layers that split easily. Like slate, the minerals in phyllite have a parallel structure. The atoms in the crystals are bonded to one another in repeating shapes. But the bonds between some atoms are weaker than others. When weak atom bonds line up inside a rock, a cleavage plane forms. These are places where the rock can split easily. Even a very hard rock can be easy to split if it has many cleavage planes.

Phyllite is usually gray, green, or black in color. It often has a slight sheen and a crinkled surface.

The Devonian Gile Mountain Formation, located in the US state of Vermont, contains phyllite.

PSEUDOTACHYLYTE

Pseudotachylyte is a type of cataclasite. It is also a fault rock. Pseudotachylyte contains rock fragments in a glassy rock matrix. This glass results from the partial melting of the rock. Pseudotachylyte can contain many different minerals. Its makeup depends on which minerals are present at the fault line. The rock is named pseudotachylyte because it looks like tachylyte, a glassy igneous rock.

EARTHQUAKES

Pseudotachylyte may form as the result of an earthquake. These events happen when energy inside the crust is released. Earthquakes often occur along fault lines. This is because tectonic plate movement creates pressure in these places. The stored energy from this pressure is released in seismic waves. Scientists use pseudotachylytes to study ancient earthquakes. The rocks provide clues about the earthquakes that formed them.

Pseudotachylyte and tachylyte have been found at Australia's Barlangi Rock, the site of a large meteorite crater.

Pseudotachylyte is typically a dark-colored rock that contains rock or mineral fragments.

QUARTZITE

Quartzite is metamorphosed sandstone or chert. It is sometimes called metaquartzite. Both sandstone and chert are sedimentary rocks. They are rich in quartz. Quartzite is also composed mainly of quartz. In fact, most quartzites are more than 90 percent quartz. This makes them valuable sources of the mineral.

The quartz in the protoliths reorganizes under heat or pressure. It forms a uniform texture with similar-sized grains. Quartzite rocks are harder than their protoliths. They are often white in color.

MOUNTAIN FORMATION

Quartzite is typically found in places where metamorphism once occurred. For example, some rocks in the Appalachian Mountains are about 1.1 billion years old. These mountains formed because of tectonic activity. The heat and pressure from their formation created quartzite deposits. These quartzite deposits are still inside the mountains today.

Quartzite is a dense, durable rock that rates 7 on the Mohs scale.

Hanging Rock State Park in North Carolina features large quartzite cliffs that jut out over the landscape.

SCHIST

There are many kinds of schist. Schist is metamorphic rock that can be easily split. It is a medium-grade metamorphic rock. At a lower grade, similar rocks become slate and phyllite. At a higher grade, they turn into gneiss. Schists form as a result of dynamic metamorphism, or motion between rocks.

Schists can consist of many different minerals. But some are more common than others. Minerals that form long, thin, layered structures are often found in schist. These structures easily split into parallel sheets.

MICA SOURCE

Schist often contains mica. This is an aluminum silicate mineral. It is found in many igneous, sedimentary, and metamorphic rocks. The molecules in mica join together in linked shapes. These form sheets of crystal. Mica's crystal structure makes it sparkly and reflective. Schists that are rich in mica share this sparkly quality. Because of its shimmer, mica is used to add shine to products such as wallpaper. Mica also conducts electricity well. It has a wide variety of uses in electronics.

Mica from schist is often used in makeup products such as eyeshadow. It adds sparkle and shine.

SERPENTINITE

Serpentinites come from rocks that are rich in iron and magnesium. These protoliths are often igneous rocks. They metamorphose through a process called serpentinization. This is an example of a chemical metamorphic process. It happens on the seafloor at the Moho. The Moho is the boundary where Earth's crust meets the mantle. Minerals such as pyroxene are commonly found there.

When tectonic plates collide at the Moho, the rocks are exposed to very hot water. The hydrogen in the water has a chemical reaction with rock minerals. They change into serpentine minerals. These minerals get their name from their green or grayish color, which resembles snakeskin.

FINDING SERPENTINITE

Today, serpentinite can be found in places where oceans used to be. Time and geological movement have

Serpentinites, which are closely related to peridotites, are known for their waxy luster and slippery texture.

exposed these tectonic plates. Exposed ocean plates are called ophiolites. Ophiolites are located in Canada, the Pacific Ocean, the Mediterranean Sea, Oman, and the US state of California. Serpentinites are easily polished. They are sometimes cut into gemstones.

SKARN

Skarn is a chemical metamorphic rock. It is sometimes called tactite. It forms when magma intrudes on existing rocks. In the case of skarn, these rocks are carbon rich and usually sedimentary.

For example, magma might flow through a limestone deposit. This magma creates veins of igneous rock. It also releases hot water into the surrounding rock. This water contains dissolved minerals and metals from the magma. As the water travels, it changes and recrystallizes surrounding rock. The result is skarn.

SKARN DEPOSITS

Skarns can consist of many different minerals. The rocks are often sources of valuable minerals, ores, and gems. Skarns that contain these materials are called skarn deposits. The Bingham Canyon Mine is a copper deposit in Utah. It is the world's largest open-pit mine. The mine's copper comes partly from skarn deposits. Copper is an essential metal for construction and electricity.

Skarns sometimes contain valuable gemstones such as garnets and sapphires.

MINING AND QUARRYING

Mining is the process of extracting minerals from Earth's crust. Quarries, or open-pit mines, are located on Earth's surface. Underground mines are accessible only through tunnels called shafts. Mining is a dangerous job. Mines must be carefully designed and engineered. They are at risk of caving in or exploding. Mining is a huge global business. In 2022, the global mining industry was worth about $2 trillion.

SLATE

Slate is metamorphosed shale. It can also be claystone or mudstone. It is a very low-grade metamorphic rock. Because the rock is lightly metamorphosed, it is very similar to shale. It can sometimes be difficult to tell the two rocks apart. Shale and slate deposits often occur close together.

Slates formed about 550 million to 400 million years ago. In high grades, shale becomes phyllite, schist, or gneiss. Like shale and phyllite, slate is easy to split into thin sheets. However, slate does not split along its sedimentary layers in the way shale does. Since it has recrystallized, slate breaks apart at its cleavage planes, where weak atom bonds line up inside a rock.

Slates are made mostly of the minerals mica, quartz, and chlorite. They may contain other minerals that influence their color. For example, slates that contain hematite are reddish, while slates that contain high amounts of chlorite appear green.

Slate is fine grained, smooth, and hard. Most slate rocks are gray in color.

ROOFING MATERIAL

Slate is popular as a roofing material. It is waterproof and durable. The rock's ability to split into sheets is also useful in construction. It can be easily shaped into long, flat roofing tiles.

DID YOU KNOW?

People once used slate rock as a writing surface. It was used to make tablets and blackboards.

Soapstone gets its name from its soft, soapy texture. It is typically gray, green, or blue in color.

SOAPSTONE

Soapstone is also called steatite. It is a type of schist made mostly from talc. The term *soapstone* can also refer to talc itself. Talc is a pale mineral usually found in metamorphic rocks. It is extremely soft, rating only 1 on the Mohs scale. It is also resistant to heat.

A ROCK FOR COOKWARE

People have used talc-rich soapstone for thousands of years. Its softness makes it easy to carve, while its heat resistant qualities make it a good material for cookware. American Indians in the western United States made soapstone cooking bowls about 8,000 years ago. People in Scandinavia did the same a few thousand years later. Soapstone was one of the first rocks to be quarried and traded.

Today, talc from soapstone is used in paint, ceramics, plastic, and other materials. It is also used to make white marking pencils. People use these to draw on things such as wood or fabric before cutting them into shapes.

The Minoans, an ancient civilization in Greece, made bowls, vases, and other objects out of steatite.

SUEVITE

Suevite is a type of impactite. It forms from shock metamorphism. This occurs when the shock of an outside event rapidly changes the surrounding rock. Suevite forms as the result of a meteorite impact. When a large object such as a meteorite hits Earth, it sends fragments flying. This forms impactites such as suevites.

SUEVITE IN CRATERS

Large meteorite impacts can create craters. These are depressions in Earth's crust. In the crater, the heat from the meteorite melts the surrounding rock. This creates a rock called tagamite.

Below the crater's surface, rocks are rapidly crushed, recrystallized, and formed inside a new matrix. This matrix is partly melted and glassy. The resulting rock is suevite. Suevites can be found wherever there are remains of a large meteorite impact.

Suevite is often called an impact breccia.

Many suevites and other impactites have been discovered in the Nördlinger Ries crater in Germany.

DID YOU KNOW?

The names of many rocks and minerals include the suffix *-ite*. It comes from a Greek term meaning "belonging to" or "from a place."

TOURMALINITE

Tourmalinite is a chemically metamorphic rock. It is rich in the mineral tourmaline. Tourmaline is a hard silicate mineral that comes in many different colors and structures. It is sometimes sold as a gemstone. Large crystals of tourmaline are especially popular for this purpose.

Tourmalinites form when hot water with dissolved minerals flows through a rock that is rich in feldspar or mica. Tourmaline replaces some of these minerals. Granite rocks are often protoliths for tourmalinite.

A LONG HISTORY

Most tourmalinites come from the Proterozoic Eon. Significant tectonic activity took place during this time. At the beginning of the eon, Earth had only one continent. Then the continent split apart into several large landmasses. Many mountain ranges formed during this time too. These conditions led to the creation of metamorphic rocks. Rocks formed during the Proterozoic Eon often have large metal and mineral deposits.

Tourmaline crystals come in a wide range of colors, including pink, green, and blue.

UNAKITE

Unakite is a chemically metamorphic rock. It forms when minerals dissolved in hot water change the surrounding rocks. Its protoliths are granite rocks. Unakite consists mainly of the minerals epidote, feldspar, and quartz. The rock has a patchy, pink-and-green appearance. It's often used as a decorative stone or gemstone.

Unakite is named after the Unaka Mountains in North Carolina and Tennessee. The rock was first discovered in this mountain range.

A TUMBLING STONE

Unakite's unique color makes it a popular tumbling stone. Rock tumbling is a hobby for rock collectors. They put rocks in a tumbler with other rocks, grit, and water. The tumbler rotates the rocks, causing friction. This speeds up the erosion process, polishing the rocks.

CONCRETE

Concrete is an anthropic, or human-made, rock. Like naturally occurring rocks, it is solid and made of minerals. But concrete is created through artificial processes. The rock is a human-made conglomerate. It consists of sand and gravel fragments inside a matrix of cement. Human-made cement consists of dust mixed with water. Today, the most common cement type is Portland cement. It uses a powder of burnt limestone and clay or burnt limestone and shale.

Concrete is known for being a sturdy, versatile building material. It often has a pale gray color.

ANTHROPIC ROCKS

Anthropic rocks are rocks made by humans. The word comes from the Greek word *anthropos*, which means "human." Some anthropic rocks are common parts of everyday life. Bricks, for instance, are anthropic rocks. So is window glass. Ceramic pottery is also a form of human-made rock. Some scientists have proposed a revised rock cycle. It would include the creation and erosion of anthropic rocks.

During construction projects, a liquid concrete mixture is poured on certain areas. The mixture hardens into concrete rock.

A COMMON ROCK

Concrete is one of the world's most common building materials. By weight, about half of all human-made things are made of concrete. Experts estimate that by 2040, the mass of concrete on Earth will be greater than the weight of all living things combined.

Intense concrete production has a major environmental impact. The materials used to make concrete must be mined from existing rocks. In addition, the process of making concrete releases carbon dioxide into the atmosphere. This traps heat and contributes to climate change.

Meteorites are divided into three groups: irons, stones, and stony irons. Iron meteorites contain mostly metal, stony meteorites contain mostly silicate minerals, and stony irons contain equal amounts of metals and silicates.

METEORITES

Objects in space have different names based on their sizes. Asteroids and meteoroids are rocky space objects that orbit the Sun. Asteroids tend to be bigger than 3.3 feet (1 m) in diameter, while meteoroids are smaller than 3.3 feet (1 m). A meteoroid or asteroid fragment that falls to Earth is called a meteorite.

METEORITES VS. EARTH ROCKS

Meteorites can introduce new types of rocks to Earth. For example, the rock chondrite does not form on Earth. The makeup of chondrites is similar to the makeup of elements in the Sun. Most meteorites that fall to Earth are chondrites.

One famous example is the Murchison meteorite. This is the name for several pieces of meteorite that fell in Australia in 1969. The meteorite's fragments contain carbon and water, which are the building blocks of life. They also contain more than 50 acids that are not found on Earth.

Today, many pieces of the Murchison meteorite are displayed in museums.

SYNROC

Synroc is a rock developed by geologists. It is sometimes called a technogenic rock. Instead of forming through the rock cycle, technogenic rocks are made using technology.

Synroc was developed by a team of scientists. Australian geologist Ted Ringwood led the team. Ringwood was known for researching Earth's mantle. He used his geological knowledge to make new tools. Ringwood helped develop hard cutting tools. He also helped create synroc in 1978.

Synroc was developed at the Lucas Heights Research Laboratories in Australia.

A ROCK FOR NUCLEAR WASTE

Synroc has a specific purpose. The rock is a container for nuclear waste. Nuclear waste is a by-product of nuclear power plants. It is radioactive. The waste emits particles that can damage the DNA of living things. DNA, or deoxyribonucleic acid, is the chemical that is the basis of genetics, through which traits are passed from parent to child. Synroc is designed to keep nuclear waste safely contained.

The minerals in synroc absorb radioactive waste. They incorporate it into their crystal structures. In this way, they trap the particles so that they are not released into the environment. The waste can then be contained in a stable, long-term way. Today, synroc is used worldwide for waste storage. It can safely store wastes such as radioactive material.

GLOSSARY

acidic
Describing a material with a pH value lower than 7.

alkaline
Describing a material with a pH value higher than 7.

atom
An extremely small building block of matter that contains protons, neutrons, and electrons.

compound
A substance made by combining two or more chemical elements together.

delta
An area of low land formed by a river as it flows into another body of water.

deposit
A natural collection of a material, often formed by natural processes.

element
A basic substance that cannot be broken down into anything simpler.

flagstone
A flat rock commonly used for paving or landscaping.

friction
The force that resists the motion of two things against each other.

groundmass
The rock that surrounds and binds clasts and phenocrysts; also called a matrix.

ion
An atom with a positive or negative electrical charge.

monolith
A large mass of one type of rock.

pH scale
A scale used to measure the acidity of a substance.

phenocryst
A large crystal embedded in the fine-grained rock matrix of an igneous rock.

plagioclase
A type of feldspar mineral that contains sodium and calcium.

quarry
An open-pit mine, or to dig or extract from an open-pit mine.

TO LEARN MORE

FURTHER READINGS

Dennie, Devin. *An Anthology of Rocks and Minerals*. DK, 2024.

Rock & Gem: The Definitive Guide to Rocks, Minerals, Gems, and Fossils. DK, 2023.

Wheeler, Jill C. *The Mineral Encyclopedia*. Abdo, 2026.

ONLINE RESOURCES

To learn more about rocks, please visit **abdobooklinks.com** or scan this QR code. These links are routinely monitored and updated to provide the most current information available.

INDEX

PHOTO CREDITS

Cover Photos: Shutterstock Images, front (diorite, dunite, moonstone, eclogite, gneiss, jade, unakite, rock salt, shale, meteorites), back (pumice, breccia); Bjoern Wylezich/Shutterstock Images, front (lapis lazuli); Dima Moroz/Shutterstock Images, back (obsidian)

Interior Photos: Shutterstock Images, 1, 3 (top), 3 (top middle), 3 (bottom middle), 3 (bottom), 4, 8, 9, 12–13, 14–15, 16, 23, 24, 24–25, 26, 28, 34–35, 38, 41, 46, 52, 54, 55, 56, 57, 58, 59, 60, 64, 65, 66, 68, 70, 70–71, 72, 72–73, 74, 75, 77, 79, 80–81 (top), 80–81 (bottom), 83, 89, 90, 92, 93, 96, 97, 102, 103, 106, 107, 108, 110–111, 112, 118, 126, 132, 134, 135, 137, 141, 144, 146, 150, 150–151, 152–153, 153, 154, 160, 162–163, 165, 167, 168, 171, 172, 178, 180, 181, 183, 184–185, 187; Baac3nes/Moment/Getty Images, 5; NASA, 6–7, 19, 49; Red Line Editorial, 11; Posnov/Moment/Getty Images, 12; Jasius/Moment/Getty Images, 14; Marli Miller/UCG/Universal Images Group/Getty Images, 17, 87, 123, 157, 161; Jon G. Fuller/VW Pics/Universal Images Group/Getty Images, 18; Soni Macy/Alamy, 20; Breck P. Kent/Shutterstock Images, 21, 32, 140; DEA/R. Appiani/De Agostini/Getty Images, 22; Sepia Times/Universal Images Group/Getty Images, 27, 69, 175; Josh Bryan/Shutterstock Images, 29; Phil Degginger/Science Source, 30, 170; Richard Newton/Alamy, 31; Dennis MacDonald/Shutterstock Images, 33; Susan E. Degginger/Science Source, 34, 98, 142; Marieke Peche/Shutterstock Images, 36; Chris Rinckes/Shutterstock Images, 36–37; Gabbro/Alamy, 39; Science Stock Photography/Science Source, 40, 84, 174; Björn Wylezich/Alamy, 42, 138; ilbusca/DigitalVision Vectors/Getty Images, 43; Dirk Wiersma/Science Source, 44; SJ Images/Alamy, 45; GoodLifeStudio/E+/Getty Images, 47; The Natural History Museum, London/Science Source, 48; Krim Kate/Shutterstock Images, 50; iStockphoto, 51; Kumar Sriskandan/Alamy, 53; Sven-Erik Arndt/Arterra/Universal Images Group/Getty Images, 60–61; Nessa Eull/GeoDIL, 62; John Lambing/Alamy, 63; Mlenny/E+/Getty Images, 66–67; petekarici/E+/Getty Images, 76; Fokin Oleg/Shutterstock Images, 78; Stefan Toonstra/Alamy, 82; Barbara Smyers/Shutterstock Images, 84–85; Siim Sepp/Alamy, 86, 131; Jose Luis Stephens/Shutterstock Images, 88–89; Science & Society Picture Library/Getty Images, 91; Robert Michael/dpa/picture alliance/Getty Images, 94; Danby Sinclair/Shutterstock Images, 95; Dylan Garcia Photography/Alamy, 99; Aleksandr Pobedimskiy/Shutterstock Images, 100; Hulton-Deutsch Collection/Corbis Historical/Getty Images, 101; PB/YB/Alamy, 104; Alvis Upitis/Pacific Stock/Image Source Limited/Alamy, 105; Westend61/Getty Images, 109; Bruce Montagne/Dembinsky Photo Associates/Alamy, 113; DK Images/Science Source, 114, 136; Jingying Zhao/Moment/Getty Images, 115; Kerry Whitworth/Alamy, 116; Donna Gibbs-Williams/Shutterstock Images, 116–117; Douglas Sacha/Moment/Getty Images, 119; Dusty Roads/Shutterstock Images, 120; Pier Marco Tacca/Getty Images News/Getty Images, 121; Patrick Gorski/NurPhoto/Getty Images, 122; José María Barres Manuel/Alamy, 124, 133; Jim West/UCG/Universal Images Group/Getty Images, 124–125; Michael LaMonica/Shutterstock Images, 127; Steve McAlister/Photographer's Choice RF/Getty Images, 128; Ed Jones/AFP/Getty Images, 129; Robert and Jean Pollock/Science Source, 130–131; Peter Menzel/Science Source, 139; chrisstockphotography/Alamy, 143; Walter Geiersperger/Corbis Documentary/Getty Images, 145; USC Pacific Asia Museum/Hulton Archive/Getty Images, 147; Bjoern Wylezich/Shutterstock Images, 148; DEA/G. Dagli Orti/De Agostini/Getty Images, 149; Mira Kos/Shutterstock Images, 155; Frank Hammerschmidt/dpa/picture alliance/Getty Images, 156; Harry Taylor/Dorling Kindersley/Science Source, 158; Liu Guoxing/Visual China Group/Getty Images, 158–159; SBS Eclectic Images/Alamy, 163; Chansak Joe/Shutterstock Images, 164–165; Rattachon Angmanee/Shutterstock Images, 166; Alan Morris/Shutterstock Images, 169; Irene Miller/Shutterstock Images, 173; Detlev Van Ravenswaay/Science Source, 176; Stefan Puchner/Süddeutsche Zeitung Photo/Alamy, 177; Cagla Acikgoz/Shutterstock Images, 179; Anton Starikov/Shutterstock Images, 182; Argonne National Laboratory/Field Museum Library/Premium Archive/Getty Images, 184; Robert Pearce/Fairfax Media Archives/Getty Images, 186

ABDOBOOKS.COM

Published by Abdo Reference, a division of ABDO, PO Box 398166, Minneapolis, Minnesota 55439. Copyright © 2026 by Abdo Consulting Group, Inc. International copyrights reserved in all countries. No part of this book may be reproduced in any form without written permission from the publisher. Encyclopedias™ is a trademark and logo of Abdo Reference.

Printed in China.
082025
012026

Editor: Laura Stickney
Series Designer: Colleen McLaren
Production Designer: Ebonee Estrella

LIBRARY OF CONGRESS CONTROL NUMBER: 2025939300

PUBLISHER'S CATALOGING-IN-PUBLICATION DATA

Names: Buckey, A. W., author.

Title: The rock encyclopedia / by A. W. Buckey

Description: Minneapolis, Minnesota: Abdo Reference, 2026 | Series: Geology encyclopedias | Includes online resources and index.

Identifiers: ISBN 9781098298913 (lib. bdg.) | ISBN 9798384932710 (ebook)

Subjects: LCSH: Rocks--Juvenile literature. | Earth sciences--Juvenile literature. | Geoscience (Geology)--Juvenile literature. | Geology--Juvenile literature. | Encyclopedias--Juvenile literature.

Classification: DDC 552--dc23